The Pocket Encyclopedia of World Aircraft in Color

BOMBERS IN SERVICE
PATROL AND TRANSPORT AIRCRAFT
Since 1960

The Pocket Encyclopedia
of World Aircraft in Color

BOMBERS IN SERVICE
PATROL AND TRANSPORT AIRCRAFT
SINCE 1960

by
KENNETH MUNSON

Illustrated by
JOHN W. WOOD

Frank Friend
Brian Hiley
William Hobson
Tony Mitchell
Jack Pelling

Revised Edition

Macmillan Publishing Co., Inc.
New York

The original volume *Bombers, Patrol
and Transport Aircraft* first published
1966 (reprinted 1967)

© 1972 Blandford Press Ltd.
Revised edition © 1975
Blandford Press Ltd.

Macmillan Publishing Co., Inc.
866 Third Avenue, New York, N.Y. 10022

Library of Congress Cataloging in Publication Data

Munson, Kenneth G
  Bombers in service.

  (Macmillan color series)
  Original ed. published in 1966 under title:
Bombers, patrol and transport aircraft.
   1. Bombers.   2. Transport planes.   3. Air-
planes, Military.   I. Wood, John W.   II. Title.
UG1242.B6M86   1975   358.4'18'3   75–14214
ISBN 0–02–587940–5

First American Edition 1972
First American revised edition 1975

Color printed by the Ysel Press, Deventer, Holland
Text printed and books bound in Great Britain by
Richard Clay (The Chaucer Press), Ltd., Bungay, Suffolk

PREFACE

When the original two volumes in this 'Pocket Encyclopaedia' were published in 1966 they were regarded as something of an experiment, and included the major aircraft types then in service, regardless of age. Since then, the original idea has given rise to a whole series of volumes to cover the major civil as well as military aircraft of the world, from the Wright *Flyer* onwards, each volume covering a convenient period of time.

When these original two titles first became due for revision, it seemed appropriate to revise them completely to cover the period from 1960 onwards, discarding earlier aircraft which would then appear in other volumes covering the period 1945–60. The effect of this was to permit the inclusion of a greater variety of contemporary aircraft, so that most of the present volume consists of new or extensively-revised material.

As usual, thanks are again due to Ian D. Huntley for his continuing advice on the matter of colours and markings. Friends or other sources who kindly made material available or provided help in other ways included, particularly, *AiReview* magazine, Mário Roberto vaz Carneiro, the British and US journals of the IPMS, Marcelo W. Miranda, Stephen Peltz, Profile Publications Ltd and John W. R. Taylor. To them also my thanks are extended.

Kenneth Munson

March 1975

5

INTRODUCTION

Broadly speaking, the aircraft described and illustrated in the companion volume on 'Fighters' are those whose duties, in operations against a hostile power, would take place within, or at a reasonably short distance from, the areas occupied by their own forces. In this volume is a further selection of warplanes, comprising those types that would be required to fly over greater distances, carrying the war back to an enemy's home ground or bringing up forces and supplies from home bases far away.

These aircraft can be separated into two basic camps, according to whether their primary function is of a strategic or a tactical nature. Webster defines a strategic role as one 'designed or trained to strike an enemy at the sources of his military, economic or political power'; and a tactical operation as one 'involving actions or means of less magnitude or at a shorter distance from a base of operations than those of strategy; of, relating to, or designed for air attack in close support of friendly ground forces'. The bombers of today can, like the fighters, be divided into a number of more specialised sub-categories, including intercontinental and medium range strategic bombers, short- and medium-range tactical bombers, night interdictors and low-level strike aircraft. Most of these normally have an internal bay for the stowage of bombs or other weapons, although the stand-off weapons carried by British, French, Russian and US strategic bombers are mounted externally or semi-externally. But a full bomb bay no longer represents necessarily the maximum capacity of most bomber aircraft. Even the giant B-52 Stratofortress, with an internal capacity of fifty-four 750 lb high-explosive bombs, has been subjected to structural reinforcement in order to carry a further quantity on pylons underneath the wings; and the FB-111A, Strategic Air Command's bomber version of the swing-wing F-111 fighter, carries this step to what may seem a ludicrous extreme by being able to carry no fewer than *forty-eight* 750 lb bombs under its wings while the actual bomb bay is occupied by only two bombs of the same modest size.

One strategic bomber, the supersonic B-58 Hustler, remained unique among serving aircraft until its retirement in 1970 in having been designed deliberately without any internal provision at all for an ordnance load. Instead it carried its total offensive load in an aerodynamic 'weapons pod' which also contained fuel for the outward half of the journey. Thus the whole pod could be released when the target was reached, leaving the Hustler 'clean' for a fast homeward run. The Hustler, incidentally, provided an interesting comparison with the Soviet Tupolev Tu-22, proving the point that aerodynamic beauty is not necessarily a complete guide to performance or capability. The Tu-22 is a far more attractive aeroplane aesthetically than the wasp-like, pod-bedecked Hustler, yet the US bomber not only had the better performance of the two but entered service several years ahead of the Tu-22.

Another inevitable comparison is that between the American B-52 and the Russian Tu-95. Both are comparable in terms of size, shape, weight and original purpose, and have been in service for a similar length of time. However, whereas the B-52 has turbojet engines (turbofans in the B-52H), the Tu-95 is powered by propeller-turbines. Admittedly these turboprops are no mean performers, but even so the Tu-95's top speed is still some 100 mph (160 km/hr) below that of the Stratofortress, and the choice of this form of powerplant for an intercontinental bomber caused the Russian aeroplane to be regarded with some scepticism when its existence first became known in the west. The passage of time, however, revealed the true value of the Tu-95 to the Soviet Union. This lay not so much in its intrinsic value as a warplane, but in the effect which the very existence of an intercontinental bomber in the Russian inventory had upon defence activity in the United States. For a relatively small cost – for the Tu-95 was developed in parallel with the Tu-114 commercial airliner – the USSR succeeded in causing the expenditure of many extra millions of dollars on advanced radar and electronic defence networks across the North American continent, not to mention the accelerated development of defensive aircraft and missile systems. Once its original purpose was achieved, the Tu-95 was switched almost exclusively to long-range land and oversea reconnaissance and early warning work, though with the stand-off weapon that it can carry it could still presumably be called into use as an intercontinental strike weapon; but this task would now most likely fall upon the new variable-geometry supersonic 'Backfire', a more recent product of the Tupolev design bureau.

British and French strategic bombers share a fundamental design advantage in that they are considerably closer geographically to their potential target. Hence, they do not have to carry anything like the quantity of fuel needed by a B-52 or a Tu-95 to reach its objective, and are consequently a great deal smaller than these giant aeroplanes. They can, however, be refuelled in flight by tanker aircraft if required to carry out missions of greater duration. The Mirage IV-A, a scaled-up development of Dassault's delta fighter, gives the Armée de l'Air a nuclear weapon carrier with a Mach 2 performance, while Britain's dwindling force of Mk 2 Vulcans attains rather less than half this speed. There is not quite the disparity in effectiveness here that might be assumed from the relative speeds of the aircraft concerned, for the bomber coming in very low – well under a thousand feet – at high subsonic speed has a better chance of eluding an enemy's ground-based early warning radar system until the very last minute, and is less vulnerable to anti-aircraft defences than a faster and higher-flying attacker. High speed at height is, however, useful over the early part of the flight, and both bombers are able to perform effectively at either high or low level. High speed at both low and high levels gives SAC's new FB-111A, with its advanced terrain-following radar, this ability to come in fast to a target at only 200 ft (60 m) altitude, virtually undetected by any ground-based radar. A larger and even more sophisticated swing-wing type, which may be regarded as the American counterpart to 'Backfire', is the Rockwell International B-1, which made its first flight in late 1974 and will eventually re-place the B-52 as the USAF's principal strategic bomber. In 1974, first reports appeared of another large Soviet bomber under develop-ment: a tandem-delta-wing design from the Sukhoi bureau. No indication of the status or capabilities of this bomber had been given at the time of closing for press.

While 1966 marked the final retirement from front-line service of the US Air Force's veteran B-47 Stratojet medium bomber, its Russian counterpart, the Tu-16, continues to soldier on with the Soviet air and naval air arms. But whereas the B-47 served no other country outside America, the Tu-16 has been supplied since 1961 to pro-Soviet key points in the Middle and Far East, the United Arab Republic and Indonesia, and those delivered to both governments were provided with Russian air-to-surface anti-shipping missiles.

Recent development of light tactical bombers in the Soviet Union has produced only one notable type (the Yakovlev Yak-28) that has yet entered service. The Yak-28 provided, after an uncommonly long gestation period, a Soviet Air Force successor to the veteran Il-28 Beagle, although there has been no evidence of its allocation to any of the numerous Beagle-equipped air forces outside of Russia. The Yak-28 represents an updating of the Il-28 concept rather than a particularly sophisticated replacement for it; and it is hardly in the same class as, say, the Hawker Siddeley Buccaneer.

Mention of the Buccaneer leads naturally to a consideration of the other carrier-based bomber aircraft now in service. As Britain's only remaining aeroplane in this category, most Buccaneers having now been transferred from the Royal Navy to the RAF, it has few parallels except in the US Navy. The Soviet naval air arm relies largely on land-based standard air force types, the Tu-16, Tu-22 and Tu-95. The Buccaneers of South Africa's Maritime Command are also deployed from bases on land. Argentina and Australia have the excellent Douglas Skyhawk, which will serve them at least into the late 1970s; but otherwise the use of bombers from carrier bases is virtually the prerogative of the United States Navy, which has a variety of such types ranging in size from the tiny Skyhawk upwards. Even here, the Vigilante has now been allocated a primary reconnaissance role in lieu of its original function. However, the Soviet Navy is known to have aircraft carriers under construction, though as yet the types of aircraft which will operate from them are unidentified.

While the bigger, faster and more expensive bombers owe their existence mainly to the threat of war on a global scale, there is another category which has been very much to the fore in the past decade or so in the all-too-frequent border incidents, minor conflicts and wars of attrition like the one in Vietnam. The aircraft in this category, mostly American in origin, are variously classed as 'commando' or 'coin' (an abbreviation of *co*unter-*in*surgency) types, and functionally they represent a logical development from what used to be called the police aeroplane or, in even earlier days, the colonial aeroplane. It was the Korean war of 1950–53 which laid the foundations of today's emphasis on the coin aircraft, and two piston-engined types in particular stand out in this field. The twin-engined B-26 Invader and the single-engined AD Skyraider, both Douglas types, were on the verge of being retired from active US service at this time, but because of the outbreak of hostilities were retained on the active list. Korea was the first full-scale military confrontation in which the opposing elements were equipped substantially with et aircraft, and much has since been written and said of the air battles between the MiG-15 on the one hand and the Meteor and Sabre on the other. This tended to overshadow the notable part played in the struggle by piston-engined aircraft, but it is a fact that, despite the arrival of more and more jet aircraft in the fighting areas, the Invader, Skyraider and others continued to be used in undiminishing numbers throughout the whole period of the war. In Algeria, the French too found that the piston engine still had advantages over the jet in certain applications, and subsequent international events have served to establish the coin aircraft as a type with a positive place in 'limited war' engagements. The Combat Applications Group of the USAF Special Air Warfare Center at Eglin Air Force Base, Florida, has given many veteran aircraft a new lease of life by modifying them for coin duties with TAC Commando Air Wings operating in Vietnam. The Skyraider, some twenty years after its Korean war service, is still one of the best coin aircraft in the business, despite the predominance nowadays of other types such as the Skyhawk and A-6 Intruder, and by more recent types such as North American Rockwell's excellent OV-10A Bronco.

This is not the place to argue the future or otherwise of the aircraft carrier as a capital ship, but one thing that brooks no argument at all is the threat presented by the existence of the missile-carrying submarine. Such a means of attack is the most difficult to detect of any yet devised, and presents the defence organisations of both east and west with a prodigious task of surveillance, not to mention that of being able to counter such an attack if it is ever launched. The needle-in-a-haystack job of locating and keeping track of surface vessels is arduous enough, but to find and follow an unseen, underwater craft from the air is a hundred times more difficult. Any aeroplane designed for such a role must have two primary attributes: the ability to stay aloft for hours at a time on patrols far away from its home base, and the space to carry a vast array of radio, radar, echo-ranging, magnetic and electronic detection equipment. It must also carry a substantial crew to man this equipment, and allow space for their 'operations room' and sleeping quarters (and, perhaps, for a relief crew if the patrol is to be an especially long one). None matches the Super Constellation's maximum complement of thirty-one crew members, but ten or a dozen are not uncommon in aircraft of this type. The modern anti-submarine patrol aircraft combines both the 'hunter' and 'killer' roles in the one airframe, carrying an assortment of sea mines, depth charges, acoustic homing torpedoes and the like with which to attack its quarry. The aircraft in this class come in many shapes and sizes, ranging from the relatively small, single-engined Alizé through the medium-sized Grumman Tracker and Lockheed Viking to larger, land-based types such as the Neptune, Orion, Atlantic, Nimrod, Argus and Il-38. The carrier-borne aircraft can afford to be smaller, of course, since they have a mobile base and do not need to cover such great distances as those operating from shore stations.

There are a growing number of types whose function is to provide airborne early warning of attack, be this from submarine, surface vessel or even land-based aircraft. These include the Mk 3 Gannet of the Fleet Air Arm and the American Tracer and Hawkeye, all distinguishable by large external radomes of various shapes and sizes. These aircraft normally carry no weapons themselves to launch any form of counter-attack, although a part of the Hawkeye's job is to remain aloft after relaying a warning to act as an aerial 'command post' directing the retaliatory force. Even larger than Hawkeye are the USSR's 'Moss' derivative of the Tu-114 and the forthcoming Boeing E-3A, based on the commercial Model 707-320B.

Early warning of possible attack is by no means the only form which modern reconnaissance takes. Fundamentally, there are at least three other categories into which reconnaissance can be subdivided: these are photographic, electronics and weather reconnaissance. The nature of photographic reconnaissance needs little elaboration here: it, and the allied art of photographic interpretation, came into their own during World War 2, and techniques have advanced significantly since then, both for military applications and in the civil fields of aerial survey and map-making. Electronics reconnaissance is that branch of reconnaissance devoted to monitoring the radio and radar transmissions of potentially hostile powers, and perhaps providing appropriate electronic countermeasures (ECM), while weather reconnaissance has obvious value to the military as well as to civilian establishments.

Speed has long been one of the prime requisites of the military reconnaissance aircraft, and for this reason many present-day PR types are converted from current fighters. However, with the advances made in modern high definition camera lenses and photographic emulsions, pictures can now be taken by relatively slow-flying machines operating at altitudes beyond the reach of most

ntercepting fighters. Even enlargements of pictures taken at a
height of 50,000 ft (15,240 m), which is not an exceptional altitude
in PR terms, can, with a resolution as precise as a hundred lines
to the millimetre, reveal features as tiny as a golf ball or as fine as the
white lines on a tennis court. The slow-but-high approach to photographic reconnaissance gave the world the notorious Lockheed
U-2, the only currently-serving military aeroplane to be designed
purely for reconnaissance work; this was virtually a jet-powered
sailplane, and had its Russian counterpart in the form of the Mandrake, an extended-span development of the Yak-25 fighter. Most
other high altitude reconnaissance within the Earth's atmosphere is
undertaken by modified versions of existing bomber aircraft, the
fighter/reconnaissance types being generally more suitable for low-
level work. Russia uses the Tu-16, Tu-95 and Tu-22; the United
States has the Martin RB-57D and RB-57F – the latter surely the
ultimate in Canberra 'stretch' – and now has, in the Mach 3 Lockheed SR-71, the world's fastest and highest-flying reconnaissance
aeroplane. Improved electronic flash equipment now facilitates
night photographic work; infra-red, especially when used in con-
junction with colour emulsions, provides an admirable means of
unmasking' camouflaged installations; and the sideways-looking
airborne radar and terrain-mapping radar, such as that carried by
the RA-5C Vigilante and the Grumman Mohawk respectively, gives
excellent coverage at low levels. An interesting variation from more
conventional practice is that provided by the drone-carrying
DC-130 Hercules which have been used in Southeast Asia. The
information is gathered by remotely controlled Ryan Firebee
drones launched from beneath the wings of the Hercules, after
which the drones are monitored back to land by parachute in pre-
selected recovery areas. The Firebee and other drone vehicles
will be heard of much more in the years ahead, as a whole new
breed of these RPVs (remotely piloted vehicles) is developed to
carry out many of the missions at present undertaken by manned
aircraft.

The Hercules, of course, versatile though it is, really belongs to the
final category covered by this volume, the field of transportation.
The world's battles are still fought out very largely by the man on
the ground, and his very existence, as well as the maintenance of his
food and equipment supplies, rely heavily on air transport backing.
In the matter of shape, size or capability, transport aircraft range

from small, single-engined types to such giants as the An-22, Il-76 StarLifter and Galaxy.

Several veterans of World War 2 continue to give yeoman service. They include – inevitably – the ageless and seemingly irreplaceable DC-3, known in military guise as the C-47, and the Fairchild C-123 Provider. Among the more modern types, the short/medium-range Caribou and Buffalo, together with transport helicopters, provide close-support transportation of and for the ground forces in the field; the ubiquitous Hercules carries many tactical loads over medium ranges; while the long-range strategic hauls are flown by the Star Lifter and Galaxy.

The Royal Air Force has two excellent strategic transports in the VC10 trooper and the Belfast freighter, the freight and troop tactical transport roles being undertaken primarily by the Andover Mks 1 and 2. Other tactical transports deserving mention are the French Noratlas, which has given way to the Hercules in some quarters and the Transall C-160 in others; and Russia's An-12, developed from civil passenger airliners of similar pattern. France's Noratlases were for many years backed by a small force of the portly Sahara; Canada has only recently retired the Yukon, a development of the Argus ASW aircraft which in turn was derived from the Britannia airliner. A more recent concept is the COD (Carrier-On-Board Delivery) transport for the provisioning of US Navy carriers at sea. This need has been met by adaptations of first the Grumman Tracker and later the Hawkeye, with enlarged fuselages for carrying cargo.

There are no vertical take-off transports yet in service, although some interesting designs are undergoing evaluation, but much design ingenuity has been exercised in shortening the take-off and landing demands of more conventional transport airframes; the Caribou and Buffalo are two excellent STOL transports which have already proved their worth in the Vietnamese operations. Military aircraft may be becoming more complex and more specialised, but at the same time they are also becoming very much more flexible, to meet the ever-changing demands of modern operational conditions.

THE COLOUR PLATES

s an aid to identification, the eighty pages of colour plates which
llow have been arranged in a basically visual order, with pro-
eller-driven aircraft first, followed by jet aircraft. The reference
umber of each aircraft corresponds to the appropriate text matter.
n index to all types appears on pages 157 to 159.

The 'split' plan view, adopted to give both upper and lower sur-
ce markings within a single plan outline, depicts the colour scheme
ppearing above and below either the port or starboard half of the
ircraft, according to whichever aspect is shown in the side eleva-
on.

The undermentioned aircraft, which appeared in the previous
dition, can now be found in the *Flying-boats and Seaplanes since 1910*
olume in this series:

Beriev Be-12
Shin Meiwa PS-1

1

Antonov An-2P of the DOSAAF, *ca* 1961-62. *Engine:* One 1,000 h.p. Shvetsov ASh-62IR nine-cylinder radial. *Span:* 59 ft. 8½ in. (18·18 m.). *Length:* 41 ft. 9½ in. (12·74 m.). *Wing area:* 769·9 sq. ft. (71·53 sq.m.). *Normal take-off weight:* 12,125 lb. (5,500 kg.). *Maximum speed:* 157 m.p.h. (253 km/hr.) at 5,750 ft. (1,750 m.). *Service ceiling:* 14,275 ft. (4,350 m.). *Range:* 560 miles (905 km.).

REGENTE (Brazil)

2

Neiva L-42 Regente of the Fôrça Aérea Brasileira, 1970. *Engine:* One 210 h.p. Continental IO-360-D six-cylinder horizontally-opposed type. *Span:* 29 ft. 11½ in. (9·13 m.). *Length:* 23 ft. 7¾ in. (7·21 m.). *Wing area:* 144·8 sq. ft. (13·45 sq. m.). *Maximum take-off weight:* 2,469 lb. (1,120 kg.). *Maximum speed:* 153 m.p.h. (246 km/hr.) at sea level. *Service ceiling:* 15,810 ft. (4,820 m.). *Maximum range:* 590 miles (950 km.).

3

Helio U-10A Super Courier of the USAF, *ca* 1965. *Engine:* One 295 h.p. Lycoming GO-480-G1D6 six-cylinder horizontally-opposed type. *Span:* 39 ft. 0 in. (11·89 m.). *Length:* 31 ft. 0 in. (9·45 m.). *Wing area:* 231·0 sq. ft. (21·46 sq. m.). *Maximum take-off weight:* 3,400 lb. (1,542 kg.). *Maximum speed:* 167 m.p.h. (269 km/hr.) at sea level. *Service ceiling:* 20,500 ft. (6,250 m.). *Range:* 660 miles (1,062 km.).

SKYRAIDER (U.S.A.)

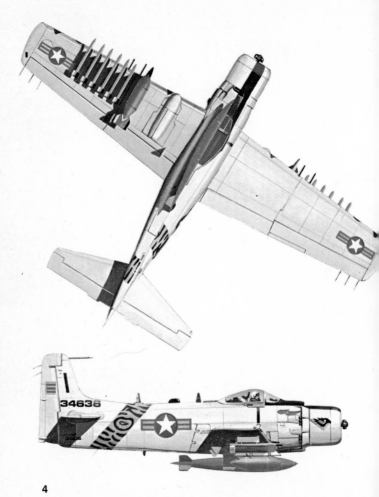

4

Douglas A-1H Skyraider of the Vietnamese Air Force, 1965. *Engine:* One 2,700 h.p. Wright R-3350-26WA eighteen-cylinder radial. *Span:* 50 ft. 0 in. (15·24 m.). *Length:* 39 ft. 2½ in. (11·95 m.). *Wing area:* 400·0 sq. ft. (37·16 sq. m.). *Maximum take-off weight:* 25,000 lb (11,340 kg.). *Maximum speed:* 285 m.p.h. (459 km/hr.) at 18,500 ft. (5,640 m.). *Service ceiling:* 28,500 ft. (8,685 m.). *Radius on internal fuel:* 1,145 miles (1,840 km.).

ALIZÉ (France)

5

Breguet 1050 Alizé of the Aéronavale, *ca* 1964. *Engine:* One 2,100 e.h.p.
Rolls-Royce Dart RDa.7 Mk 21 turboprop. *Span:* 51 ft. $2\frac{1}{4}$ in. (15·60 m.).
Length: 45 ft. $5\frac{3}{4}$ in. (13·86 m.). *Wing area:* 387·5 sq. ft. (36·00 sq. m.).
Normal take-off weight: 18,100 lb. (8,210 kg.). *Maximum speed:* 282 m.p.h.
(454 km/hr.) at 10,000 ft. (3,050 m.). *Service ceiling:* 26,250 ft. (8,000
m.). *Maximum range:* 1,324 miles (2,130 km.).

GANNET (U.K.)

6

Westland (Fairey) Gannet AEW.Mk 3 of No. 849 Squadron Royal Navy, on detachment on board HMS *Ark Royal, ca* 1961. *Engine:* One 3,875 e.h.p. Bristol Siddeley Double Mamba 102 turboprop. *Span:* 54 ft. 7 in. (16·64 m.); *folded,* 20 ft. 0 in. (6·10 m.). *Length:* 43 ft. 11 in. (13·39 m.). *Wing area:* 490·0 sq. ft. (45·52 sq. m.). *Maximum take-off weight:* approx. 24,000 lb. (10,886 kg.). *Maximum speed:* 250 m.p.h. (402 km/hr.) at 5,000 ft. (1,525 m.). *Service ceiling:* 25,000 ft. (7,620 m.). *Range with underwing fuel tanks:* approx. 800 miles (1,285 km.).

CESSNA O-2 (U.S.A.)

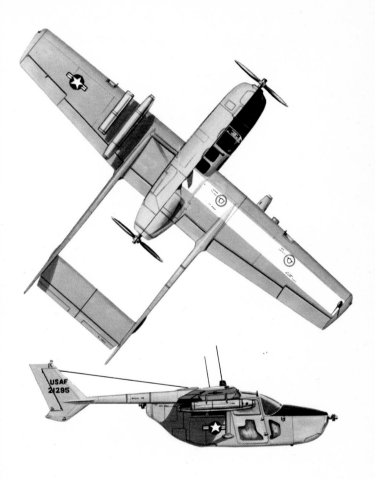

7

Cessna O-2A (Forward Air Controller's aircraft) of the USAF, 1968-69.
Engines: Two 210 h.p. Continental IO-360-C six-cylinder horizontally-opposed
type. *Span:* 38 ft. 2 in. (11·63 m.). *Length:* 29 ft. 9 in. (9·07 m.). *Wing
area:* 202·5 sq. ft. (18·81 sq. m.). *Take-off weight:* 4,300 lb. (1,950 kg.).
Maximum speed: 199 m.p.h. (320 km/hr.) at sea level. *Service ceiling:* 18,000
ft. (5,490 m.). *Maximum range, standard fuel:* 755 miles (1,215 km.).

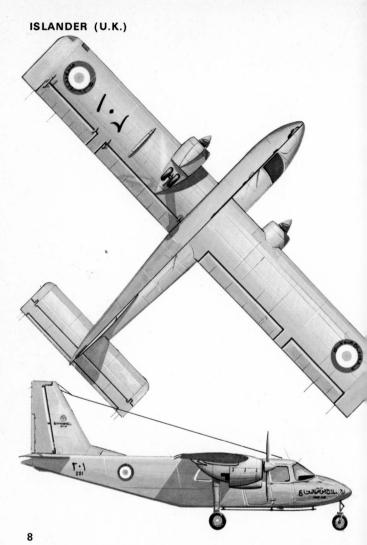

ISLANDER (U.K.)

8

Britten-Norman BN-2A Defender of the Abu Dhabi Defence Force, early 1968.
Engines: Two 300 h.p. Lycoming IO-540-K1B5 six-cylinder horizontally-opposed type. *Span:* 49 ft. 0 in. (14·94 m.). *Length:* 35 ft. 7¾ in. (10·86 m.). *Wing area:* 325·0 sq. ft. (30·19 sq. m.). *Maximum take-off weight:* 6,600 lb. (2,993 kg.). *Maximum speed:* 176 m.p.h. (283 km/hr.) at sea level. *Service ceiling:* 17,000 ft. (5,180 m.). *Maximum range on internal fuel:* 1,260 miles (2,027 km.).

24

PIAGGIO P166M (Italy)

9

Piaggio P.166M of the Aeronautica Militare Italiano, *ca* 1962. *Engines:* Two 340 h.p. Lycoming GSO-480-B1C6 six-cylinder horizontally-opposed type. *Span:* 46 ft. 9 in. (14·25 m.). *Length:* 38 ft. 0¾ in. (11·60 m.). *Wing area:* 285·9 sq. ft. (26·56 sq. m.). *Maximum take-off weight:* 8,113 lb. (3,680 kg.). *Maximum speed:* 223 m.p.h. (359 km/hr.). *Service ceiling:* 25,500 ft. (7,770 m.). *Maximum range:* 1,290 miles (2,080 km.).

MITSUBISHI MU-2 (Japan)

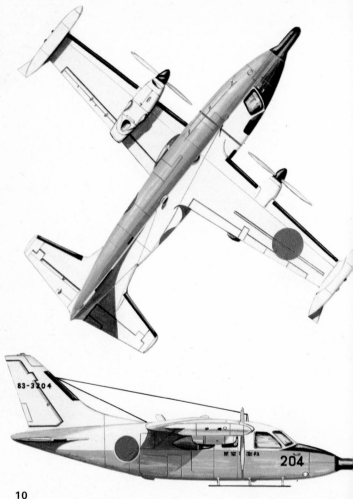

10

Mitsubishi MU-2E of the Japan Air Self-Defence Force, 1969. *Engines:* Two 605 e.h.p. AiResearch TPE 331-25A/25B turboprops. *Span:* 39 ft. 2 in. (11·94 m.). *Length:* 35 ft. 1¼ in. (10·70 m.). *Wing area:* 178·1 sq. ft. (16·55 sq. m.). *Maximum take-off weight:* 10,030 lb. (4,550 kg.). *Maximum cruising speed:* 310 m.p.h. (500 km/hr.) at 10,000 ft. (3,050 m.). *Service ceiling:* 25,925 ft. (7,900 m.). *Maximum range:* 1,550 miles (2,495 km.).

BASSET (U.K.)

11

Beagle Basset CC.Mk 1 of Southern Communications Squadron RAF, 1968.
Engines: Two 310 h.p. Rolls-Royce Continental GIO-470-A six-cylinder horizontally-opposed type. *Span:* 45 ft. 9½ in. (13·96 m.). *Length:* 33 ft. 3 in. (10·13 m.). *Wing area:* 214·0 sq. ft. (19·90 sq. m.). *Maximum take-off weight:* 7,500 lb. (3,402 kg.). *Maximum cruising speed:* 207 m.p.h. (333 km/hr.) at 10,000 ft. (3,050 m.). *Service ceiling:* 17,500 ft. (5,330 m.). *Range with payload of 950 lb. (431 kg.):* 1,175 miles (1,890 km.).

27

BEECHCRAFT U-21 (U.S.A.)

12

Beechcraft RU-21D of the US Army, Southeast Asia 1970. *Engines:* Two 550 s.h.p. United Aircraft of Canada PT6A-20 turboprops. *Span:* 45 ft. 10½ in. (13·98 m.). *Length:* 35 ft. 6 in. (10·82 m.). *Wing area:* 279·7 sq. ft. (25·98 sq. m.). *Maximum take-off weight:* 9,650 lb. (4,377 kg.). *Maximum cruising speed:* 245 m.p.h. (395 km/hr.) at 10,000 ft. (3,050 m.). *Service ceiling:* 25,500 ft. (7,775 m.). *Typical range:* 1,167 miles (1,878 km.).

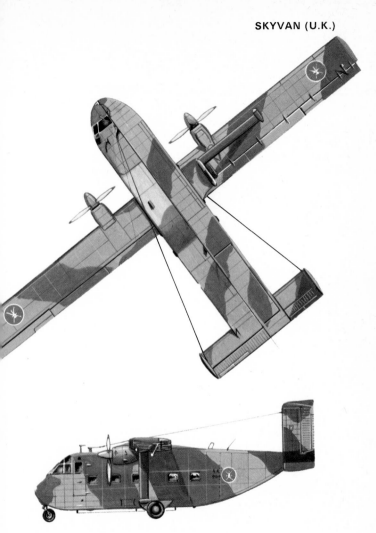

13

Shorts Skyvan Series 3M of the Sultan of Oman's Air Force, 1972. *Engines:* Two 715 s.h.p. AiResearch TPE 331-201 turboprops. *Span:* 64 ft. 11 in. (19·79 m.). *Length:* 40 ft. 1 in. (12·21 m.). *Wing area:* 373·0 sq. ft. (34·65 sq. m.). *Maximum normal take-off weight:* 13,700 lb. (6,214 kg.). *Maximum cruising speed:* 203 m.p.h. (327 km/hr.) at 10,000 ft. (3,050 m.). *Service ceiling:* 22,000 ft. (6,705 m.). *Typical range with payload of 5,000 lb. (2,268 kg.):* 240 miles (386 km.).

AVIOCAR (Spain)

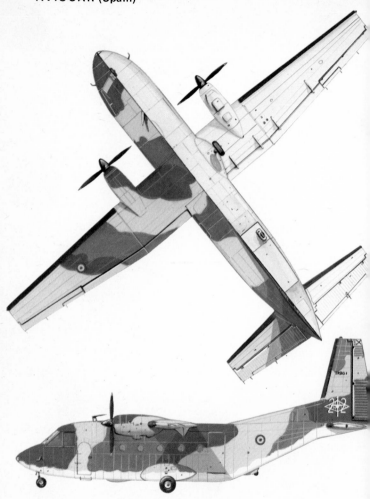

14

CASA 212 Aviocar, first pre-production aircraft in the insignia of the Ejercito del Aire, 1973. *Engines:* Two 776 e.h.p. AiResearch TPE 331-5-251 C turbo-props. *Span:* 62 ft. 4 in. (19·00 m.). *Length:* 49 ft. 10½ in. (15·20 m.). *Wing area:* 430·6 sq. ft. (40·00 sq. m.). *Maximum take-off weight:* 13,889 lb. (6,300 kg.). *Maximum cruising speed:* 223 m.p.h. (359 km/hr.) at 12,000 ft. (3,660 m.). *Service ceiling:* 28,025 ft. (8,540 m.). *Range with maximum payload of 4,410 lb. (2,000 kg.):* 298 miles (480 km.).

15

CASA 207-A (T.7A) Azor of the Ejército del Aire, *ca* 1961. *Engines:* Two
2,040 h.p. Bristol Hercules 730 fourteen-cylinder radials. *Span:* 91 ft. 2½
in. (27·80 m.). *Length:* 68 ft. 5 in. (20·85 m.). *Wing area:* 923·2 sq. ft.
(85·80 sq. m.). *Maximum take-off weight:* 36,375 lb. (16,500 kg.). *Maximum
cruising speed:* 249 m.p.h. (400 km/hr.) at 12,340 ft. (3,760 m.). *Service
ceiling:* 26,250 ft. (8,000 m.). *Range with 30 passengers:* 1,620 miles (2,610
km.).

SKYTRAIN (U.S.A.)

16

Douglas C-47A Skytrain of Eskadrille 721, Royal Danish Flyvevåbnet, *ca* 1964. *Engines:* Two 1,200 h.p. Pratt & Whitney R-1830-90C·Twin Wasp fourteen-cylinder radials. *Span:* 95 ft. 0 in. (28·96 m.). *Length:* 64 ft. 5½ in. (19·65 m.). *Wing area:* 987·0 sq. ft. (91·70 sq. m.). *Normal take-off weight:* 26,000 lb. (11,793 kg.). *Maximum speed:* 229 m.p.h. (368 km/hr.) at 7,500 ft. (2,285 m.). *Service ceiling:* 24,000 ft. (7,315 m.). *Normal range:* 1,500 miles (2,415 km.).

TROOPSHIP (Netherlands)

17

Fokker-VFW F 27 Mk 400M Troopship of the Sudan Air Force, 1966. *Engines:*
Two 2,140 s.h.p. plus 525 lb. (238 kg.) st Rolls-Royce Dart RDa.7 Mk 532-7R
turboprops. *Span:* 95 ft. 2 in. (29.00 m.). *Length:* 77 ft. 3½ in. (23.56 m.).
Wing area: 753.5 sq. ft. (70.00 sq. m.). *Maximum take-off weight:* 45,000
lb. (20,410 kg.). *Normal cruising speed:* 298 m.p.h. (480 km/hr.). at 20,000
ft. (6,100 m.). *Service ceiling:* 29,500 ft. (8,990 m.). *Operational radius:*
719 miles (1,158 km.).

GII (Argentina)

18

FMA IA 50 GII of the I Brigada Aérea, Fuerza Aérea Argentina, 1968. *Engines:* Two 930 s.h.p. Turboméca Bastan VI-A turboprops. *Span:* 64 ft. 3½ in. (19·59 m.) without tip-tanks. *Length:* 50 ft. 2½ in. (15·30 m.). *Wing area:* 450·0 sq. ft. (41·81 sq. m.). *Maximum take-off weight:* 17,085 lb. (7,750 kg.). *Maximum cruising speed:* 305 m.p.h. (491 km/hr.). *Service ceiling:* 41,000 ft. (12,500 m.). *Range with maximum payload of 3,307 lb. (1,500 kg.):* 1,240 miles (1,995 km.).

BANDEIRANTE (Brazil)

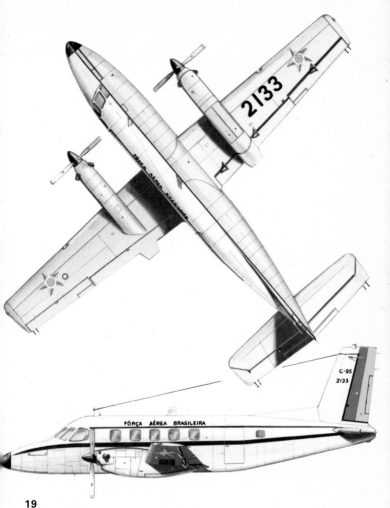

19

EMBRAER EMB-110 Bandeirante in the insignia of the Fôrça Aérea Brasileira.
Engines: Two 680 s.h.p. United Aircraft of Canada PT6A-27 turboprops. *Span:*
50 ft. 3¼ in. (15·32 m.). *Length:* 46 ft. 8¼ in. (14·23 m.). *Wing area:* 312·2
sq. ft. (29·00 sq. m.). *Maximum take-off weight:* 11,684 lb. (5,300 kg.).
Maximum cruising speed: 267 m.p.h. (430 km/hr.) at 10,000 ft. (3,050 m.).
Service ceiling: 28,400 ft. (8,660 m.). *Maximum range:* 1,289 miles (2,075
km.).

CARIBOU (Canada)

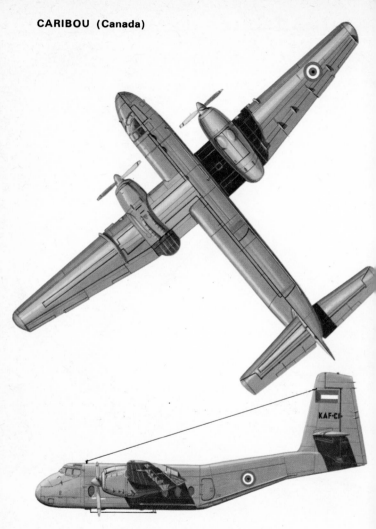

20

de Havilland Canada DHC-4 Caribou of the Kuwait Air Force, *ca* 1966. *Engines:* Two 1,450 h.p. Pratt & Whitney R-2000-7M2 fourteen-cylinder radials. *Span:* 95 ft. 7½ in. (29·15 m.). *Length:* 72 ft. 7 in. (22·13 m.). *Wing area:* 912·0 sq. ft. (84·72 sq. m.). *Normal maximum take-off weight:* 28,500 lb. (12,928 kg.). *Maximum cruising speed:* 182 m.p.h. (293 km/hr.) at 7,500 ft. (2,285 m.). *Service ceiling:* 24,800 ft. (7,560 m.). *Range with maximum payload of 8,740 lb. (3,965 kg.):* 242 miles (390 km.).

BUFFALO (Canada)

21

de Havilland Canada DHC-5 (C-8A) Buffalo of the US Army, *ca* 1965. *Engines:* Two 2,850 e.h.p. General Electric T64-GE-10 turboprops. *Span:* 96 ft. 0 in. (29·26 m.). *Length:* 77 ft. 4 in. (23·57 m.). *Wing area:* 945·0 sq. ft. (87·80 sq. m.). *Maximum take-off weight:* 38,000 lb. (17,237 kg.). *Maximum cruising speed:* 271 m.p.h. (435 km/hr.) at 10,000 ft. (3,050 m.). *Service ceiling:* 30,000 ft. (9,150 m.). *Range with maximum payload of 13,843 lb. (6,279 kg.):* 507 miles (815 km.).

PROVIDER (U.S.A.)

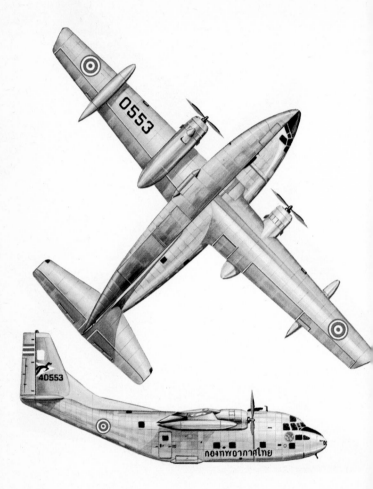

22

Fairchild C-123B Provider of the Royal Thai Air Force, *ca* 1967-68. *Engines:* Two 2,500 h.p. Pratt & Whitney R-2800-99W Double Wasp eighteen-cylinder radials. *Span:* 110 ft. 0 in. (33·53 m.). *Length:* 76 ft. 3 in. (23·24 m.). *Wing area:* 1,223·0 sq. ft. (113·62 sq. m.). *Maximum take-off weight:* 60,000 lb. (27,216 kg.). *Maximum cruising speed:* 205 m.p.h. (330 km/hr.) at 5,000 ft. (1,525 m.). *Service ceiling:* 29,000 ft. (8,840 m.). *Range with payload of 16,000 lb. (7,257 kg.):* 1,650 miles (3,380 km.).

AERITALIA G222 (Italy)

23

Aeritalia G222, second prototype in the insignia of the Aeronautica Militare Italiano, 1972-73. *Engines:* Two 3,400 s.h.p. Fiat-built General Electric T64-P4D turboprops. *Span:* 94 ft. 6 in. (28·80 m.). *Length:* 74 ft. 5½ in. (22·70 m.). *Wing area:* 882·6 sq. m. (82·00 sq. m.). *Maximum take-off weight:* 58,422 lb. (26,500 kg.). *Cruising speed:* 224 m.p.h. (360 km/hr.) at 14,750 ft. (4,500 m.). *Service ceiling:* 29,525 ft. (9,000 m.). *Range with payload of 11,025 lb (5,000 kg.):* 1,833 miles (2,950 km.).

ANDOVER (U.K.)

24

Hawker Siddeley Andover C. Mk 1 of No. 46 Squadron, RAF Transport Command, 1968. *Engines:* Two 3,245 e.h.p. Rolls-Royce Dart RDa.12 Mk 201 turboprops. *Span:* 98 ft. 3 in. (29·95 m.). *Length:* 78 ft. 0 in. (23·77 m.). *Wing area:* 831·4 sq. ft. (77·20 sq. m.). *Maximum take-off weight:* 50,000 lb. (22,680 kg.). *Maximum cruising speed:* 265 m.p.h. (426 km/hr.) at 15,000 ft. (4,750 m.). *Service ceiling:* 24,000 ft. (7,300 m.). *Range with payload of 8,530 lb. (3,870 kg.):* 1,158 miles (1,865 km.).

TRANSALL C-160 (Germany/France)

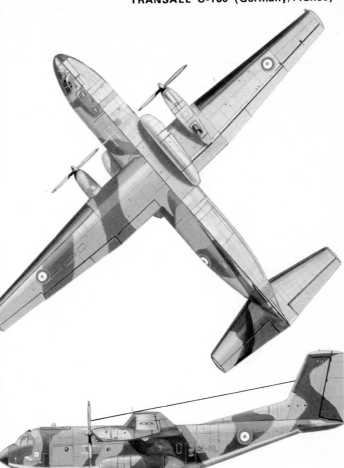

25

Transall C-160 F of the 61e Escadre, Armée de l'Air, Orléans-Bricy, 1969. *Engines:* Two 6,100 e.h.p. Rolls-Royce Tyne RTy.20 Mk 22 turboprops. *Span:* 131 ft. 3 in. (40·00 m.). *Length:* 106 ft. 3½ in. (32·40 m.). *Wing area:* 1,722·7 sq. ft. (160·10 sq. m.). *Maximum take-off weight:* 112,440 lb. (51,000 kg.). *Maximum cruising speed:* 319 m.p.h. (513 km/hr.) at 18,050 ft. (5,500 m.). *Service ceiling:* 27,900 ft. (8,500 m.). *Range with payload of 17,640 lb. (8,000 kg.):* 2,832 miles (4,558 km.).

GREYHOUND (U.S.A.)

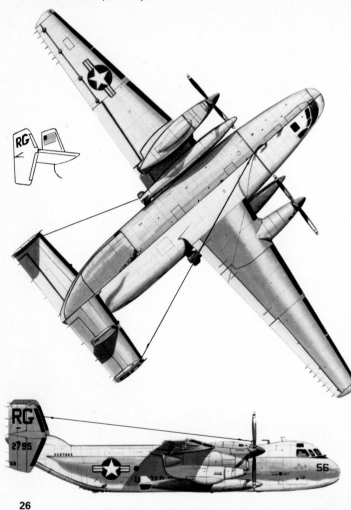

26

Grumman C-2A Greyhound of US Navy Squadron VRC-50, *ca* 1968. *Engines:* Two 4,050 e.h.p. Allison T56-A-8/8A turboprops. *Span:* 80 ft. 7 in. (24·56 m.). *Length:* 56 ft. 8 in. (17·27 m.). *Wing area:* 700·0 sq. ft. (65·03 sq. m.). *Maximum take-off weight:* 54,830 lb. (24,870 kg.). *Maximum speed:* 352 m.p.h. (567 km/hr.) at optimum altitude. *Service ceiling:* 28,800 ft. (8,870 m.). *Typical range:* 1,650 miles (2,660 km.).

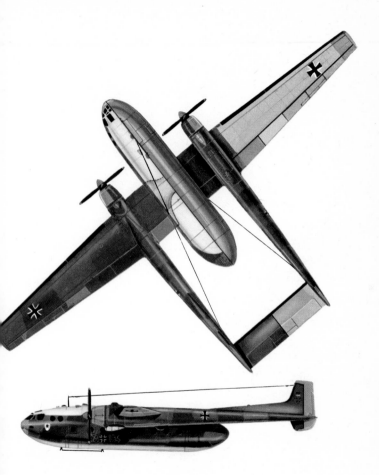

27

Nord 2501 Noratlas of Lufttransportgeschwader 61, Federal German Luftwaffe,
ca 1964. *Engines:* Two 2,040 h.p. SNECMA (Bristol) Hercules 758 fourteen-
cylinder radials. *Span:* 106 ft. 7½ in. (32·50 m.). *Length:* 72 ft. 0½ in. (21·96
m.). *Wing area:* 1,089·0 sq. ft. (101·20 sq. m.). *Maximum take-off weight:*
45,415 lb. (20,600 kg.). *Cruising speed:* 208 m.p.h. (335 km/hr.) at 9,840
ft. (3,000 m.). *Service ceiling:* 24,600 ft. (7,500 m.). *Range with payload
of 14,990 lb. (6,800 kg.):* 1,710 miles (2,750 km.).

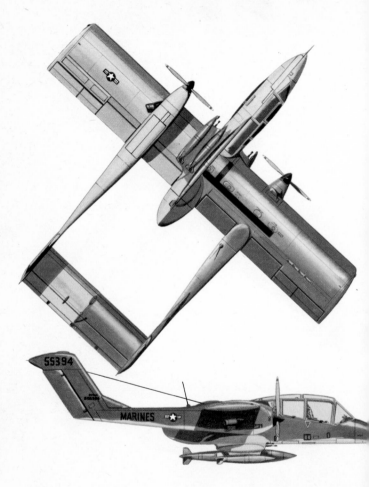

28

North American OV-10A Bronco of the US Marine Corps, *ca* 1968. *Engines:* Two 715 e.h.p. AiResearch T76-G-410/411 turboprops. *Span:* 40 ft. 0 in. (12·19 m.). *Length:* 41 ft. 7 in. (12·67 m.). *Wing area:* 291·0 sq. ft. (27·03 sq. m.). *Normal take-off weight (clean):* 9,908 lb. (4,494 kg.). *Maximum speed:* 281 m.p.h. (452 km/hr.) at sea level. *Combat radius with maximum ordnance:* 228 miles (367 km.).

29

Grumman OV-1B Mohawk of the US Army, 1966. *Engines:* Two 1,150 s.h.p.
Lycoming T53-L-15 turboprops. *Span:* 48 ft. 0 in. (14·63 m.). *Length:* 41
ft. 0 in. (12·50 m.) excluding SLAR pod. *Wing area:* 360·0 sq. ft. (33·45
sq. m.). *Maximum take-off weight:* 19,230 lb. (8,722 kg.). *Maximum speed:*
297 m.p.h. (478 km/hr.) at 5,000 ft. (1,525 m.). *Service ceiling:* 30,300
ft. (9,235 m.). *Maximum range with underwing fuel tanks:* 1,230 miles (1,980
km.).

TRACKER (U.S.A.)

30

Grumman S-2A Tracker of No. 2 Squadron, Koninklijke Marine Luchtvaart-
dienst, *ca* 1964-65. *Engines:* Two 1,525 h.p. Wright R-1820-82WA Cyclone
nine-cylinder radials. *Span:* 69 ft. 8 in. (21·23 m.). *Length:* 42 ft. 3 in.
(12·88 m.). *Wing area:* 485·0 sq. ft. (45·06 sq. m.). *Maximum take-off weight:*
26,300 lb. (11,930 kg.). *Maximum speed:* 287 m.p.h. (462 km/hr.) at sea
level. *Service ceiling:* 23,000 ft. (7,000 m.). *Maximum range:* 900 miles (1,450
km.).

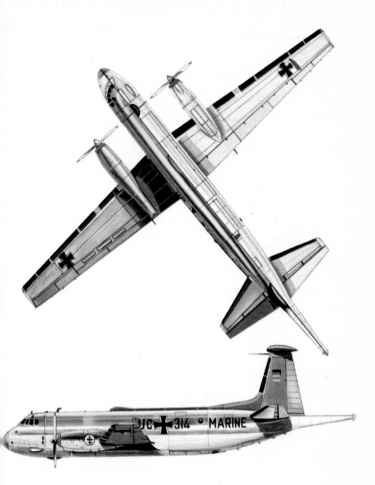

31

Breguet 1150 Atlantic of Marinefliegergruppe 3, Bundesmarine, *ca* 1967.
Engines: Two 6,106 e.h.p. SNECMA-built Rolls-Royce Tyne RTy.20 Mk 21
turboprops. *Span:* 119 ft. 1 in. (36·30 m.). *Length:* 104 ft. 2 in. (31·75
m.). *Wing area:* 1,295·0 sq. ft. (120·34 sq. m.). *Maximum take-off weight:*
95,900 lb. (43,500 kg.). *Cruising speed:* 345 m.p.h. (556 km/hr.). *Service
ceiling:* 32,800 ft. (10,000 m.). *Maximum range:* 5,590 miles (9,000 km.).

HAWKEYE (U.S.A.)

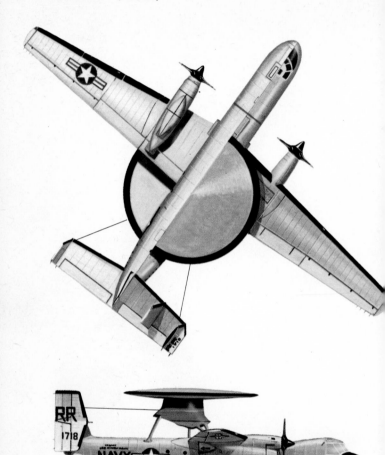

32

Grumman E-2A Hawkeye of US Navy Squadron VAW-111 (Detachment C),
USS *Kitty Hawk, ca* 1967. *Engines:* Two 4,050 e.h.p. Allison T56-A-8/8A
turboprops. *Span:* 80 ft. 7 in. (24·56 m.). *Length:* 56 ft. 4 in. (17·17 m.).
Wing area: 700·0 sq. ft. (65·03 sq. m.). *Maximum take-off weight:* 49,638
lb. (22,515 kg.). *Cruising speed:* 315 m.p.h. (508 km/hr.). *Service ceiling:*
31,700 ft. (9,660 m.). *Ferry range on internal fuel:* 1,905 miles (3,065 km.).

NEPTUNE (U.S.A.)

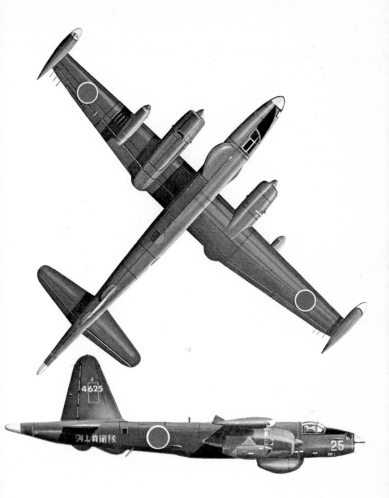

33

Kawasaki-built Lockheed P-2H (P2V-7) of the Japan Maritime Self-Defence Force, *ca* 1962. *Engines:* Two 3,500 h.p. R-3350-32W Turbo-Compounds and two 3,400 lb. (1,542 kg.) st. Westinghouse J34-WE-36 auxiliary turbojets. *Span over tip-tanks:* 103 ft. 10 in. (31·65 m.). *Length:* 91 ft. 8 in. (27·94 m.). *Wing area:* 1,000·0 sq. ft. (92·90 sq. m.). *Maximum take-off weight:* 79,895 lb. (36,240 kg.). *Maximum speed:* 356 m.p.h. (573 km/hr.) at 10,000 ft. (3,050 m.). *Service ceiling:* 22,000 ft. (6,700 m.). *Normal range:* 2,200 miles (3,540 km.).

ORION (U.S.A.)

34

Lockheed P-3A Orion of US Navy Squadron VP-46, NAS Moffett Field, California, *ca* 1964. *Engines:* Four 4,500 e.h.p. Allison T56-A-10W turboprops. *Span:* 99 ft. 8 in. (30·37 m.). *Length:* 116 ft. 10 in. (35·61 m.). *Wing area:* 1,300·0 sq. ft. (120·77 sq. m.). *Maximum take-off weight:* 134,000 lb. (60,780 kg.). *Cruising speed:* 403 m.p.h. (650 km/hr.) at 25,000 ft. (7,620 m.). *Service ceiling:* 27,000 ft. (8,230 m.). *Operational radius:* 1,550 miles (2,495 km.).

ARGUS (Canada)

35

Canadair CP-107 Argus Mk 2 of Maritime Air Command, Royal Canadian Air Force, *ca* 1962. *Engines:* Four 3,400 h.p. (3,700 h.p. with water injection) Wright R-3350-EA-1 Turbo-Compounds. *Span:* 142 ft. $3\frac{1}{2}$ in. (43·37 m.). *Length:* 128 ft. $9\frac{1}{2}$ in. (39·26 m.). *Wing area:* 2,075·0 sq. ft. (192·78 sq. m.). *Normal take-off weight:* 148,000 lb. (67,130 kg.). *Maximum speed:* 315 m.p.h. (507 km/hr.) at 20,000 ft. (6,100 m.). *Service ceiling:* 25,700 ft. (7,835 m.). *Maximum range:* 5,900 miles (9,495 km.).

ILYUSHIN II-38 (U.S.S.R.)

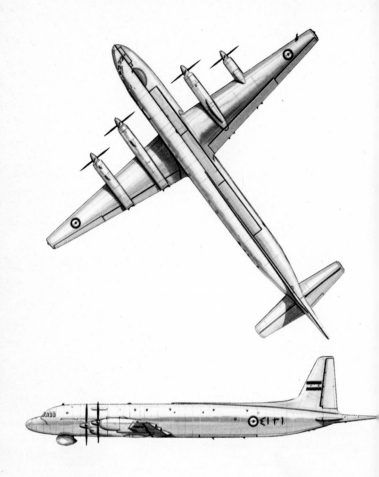

36

Ilyushin II-38 in Egyptian Air Force insignia, *ca* 1972. *Engines:* Four 4,250 e.h.p. Ivchenko AI-20M turboprops. *Span:* 122 ft. 8½ in. (37·40 m.). *Length:* 129 ft. 10 in. (39·60 m.). *Wing area:* 1,506·9 sq. ft. (140·00 sq. m.). *Maximum take-off weight:* approx. 140,000 lb. (63,500 kg.). *Maximum cruising speed:* approx. 400 m.p.h. (645 km/hr.) at 15,000 ft. (4,570 m.). *Maximum range:* approx. 4,500 miles (7,250 km.).

SUPER CONSTELLATION (U.S.A.)

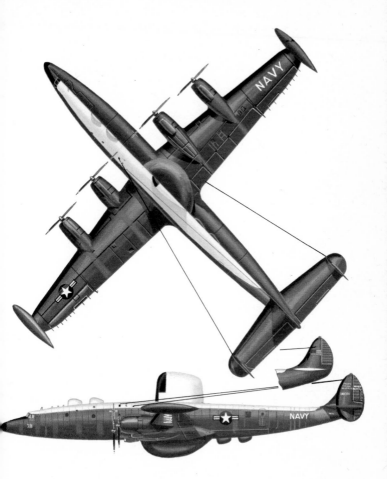

37

Lockheed EC-121K Super Constellation of the US Navy Pacific Missile Range Squadron, Hawaii, *ca* 1963. *Engines:* Four 3,400 h.p. Wright R-3350-34 or -42 Turbo-Compounds. *Span:* 123 ft. 5 in. (37·62 m.). *Length:* 116 ft. 2 in. (35·41 m.). *Wing area:* 1,654·0 sq. ft. (153·66 sq. m.). *Maximum take-off weight:* 143,600 lb. (65,135 kg.). *Maximum speed:* 321 m.p.h. (517 km/hr.) at 20,000 ft. (6,100 m.). *Service ceiling:* 20,600 ft. (6,280 m.). *Maximum range:* 4,600 miles (7,405 km.).

ARGOSY (U.K.)

38

Hawker Siddeley Argosy C.Mk 1 of No. 267 Squadron, RAF Transport Command, *ca* 1964-65. *Engines:* Four 2,680 e.h.p. Rolls-Royce Dart RDa.8 Mk 101 turboprops. *Span:* 115 ft. 0 in. (35·05 m.). *Length:* 89 ft. 2 in. (27·18 m.). *Wing area:* 1,458·0 sq. ft. (135·45 sq. m.). *Normal take-off weight:* 97,000 lb. (44,000 kg.). *Maximum cruising speed:* 269 m.p.h. (433 km/hr.) at 20,000 ft. (6,100 m.). *Range with payload of 20,000 lb. (9,072 kg.):* 1,070 miles (1,720 km.).

BELFAST (U.K.)

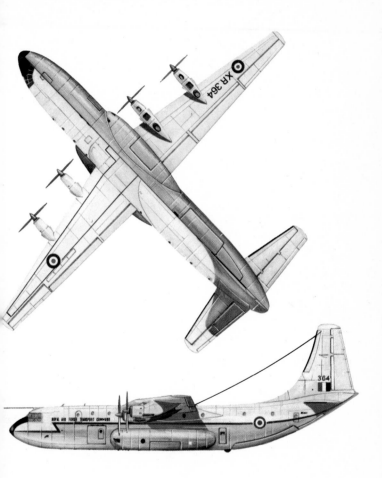

39

Shorts Belfast C. Mk 1 of No. 53 Squadron, RAF Transport Command, *ca* 1964. *Engines:* Four 5,730 e.h.p. Rolls-Royce Tyne RTy.12 Mk 101 turboprops. *Span:* 158 ft. 9½ in. (48·42 m.). *Length:* 136 ft. 5 in. (41·69 m.). *Wing area:* 2,466·0 sq. ft. (229·10 sq. m.). *Maximum take-off weight:* 230,000 lb. (104,300 kg.). *Maximum cruising speed:* 352 m.p.h. (566 km/hr.) at 24,000 ft. (7,300 m.). *Service ceiling:* 30,000 ft. (9,145 m.). *Range with maximum payload of 78,000 lb. (35,400 kg.):* 1,000 miles (1,610 km.).

40

Lockheed C-130E Hercules of the 778th Tactical Airlift Squadron, 464th Tactical Airlift Wing, USAF, Southeast Asia 1968. *Engines:* Four 4,050 e.h.p. Allison T56-A-7 turboprops. *Span:* 132 ft. 7 in. (40·41 m.). *Length:* 97 ft. 9 in. (29·78 m.). *Wing area:* 1,745·0 sq. ft. (162·12 sq. m.). *Maximum normal take-off weight:* 155,000 lb. (70,310 kg.). *Maximum cruising speed:* 368 m.p.h. (592 km/hr.). *Service ceiling:* 23,000 ft. (7,010 m.). *Maximum range with payload of 20,000 lb. (9,072 kg.):* 4,700 miles (7,560 km.).

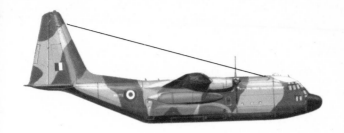

41

Lockheed Hercules C. Mk 1 (C-130K) of No. 242 OCU, RAF Transport Command, Thorney Island 1967. *Engines:* Four 4,500 e.h.p. (limited) Allison T56-A-15 turboprops. *Span, Length, Wing area and Maximum normal take-off weight:* As for C-130E. *Maximum cruising speed:* 375 m.p.h. (603 km/hr.). *Service ceiling:* 33,000 ft. (10,060 m.). *Range with maximum payload of 45,525 lb. (20,650 kg.):* 2,450 miles (3,945 km.).

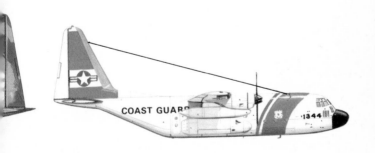

42

Lockheed HC-130B Hercules of the US Coast Guard Station, Elizabeth City, as displayed at the Paris Air Show, June 1971. *Engines, Span, Length and Wing area:* As for C-130E. *Maximum normal take-off weight:* 135,000 lb. (61,235 kg.). *Maximum cruising speed:* 370 m.p.h. (595 km/hr.). *Range/endurance:* 8-hour patrol at 1,000 miles (1,610 km.) from base.

CARGOMASTER (U.S.A.)

43

Douglas C-133B Cargomaster of Military Airlift Command, USAF, *ca* 1966. *Engines:* Four 7,500 e.h.p. Pratt & Whitney T34-P-9W turboprops. *Span:* 179 ft. 8 in. (54·76 m.). *Length:* 157 ft. 6½ in. (48·02 m.). *Wing area:* 2,673·0 sq. ft. (248·33 sq. m.). *Maximum take-off weight:* 286,000 lb. (129,725 kg.). *Maximum cruising speed:* 323 m.p.h. (520 km/hr.) at 26,850 ft. (8,185 m.). *Service ceiling:* 29,950 ft. (9,130 m.). *Range with payload of 51,850 lb. (23,518 kg.):* 4,030 miles (6,485 km.).

ANTONOV An-12 (U.S.S.R.)

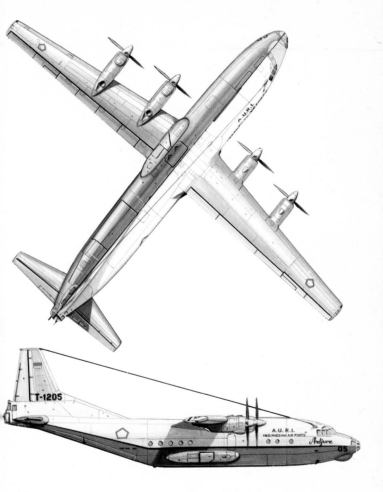

44

Antonov An-12 of the Angkatan Udara Republik Indonesia, spring 1972. *Engines:* Four 3,945 e.h.p. Ivchenko AI-20K turboprops. *Span:* 124 ft. 8 in. (38·00 m.). *Length:* 108 ft. 7¼ in. (33·10 m.). *Wing area:* 1,310·3 sq. ft. (121·73 sq. m.). *Maximum take-off weight:* 134,482 lb. (61,000 kg.). *Maximum cruising speed:* 360 m.p.h. (580 km/hr.). *Service ceiling:* 33,500 ft. (10,200 m.). *Range with maximum payload of 44,090 lb. (20,000 kg.):* 2,236 miles (3,600 km.).

ANTONOV An-22 (U.S.S.R.)

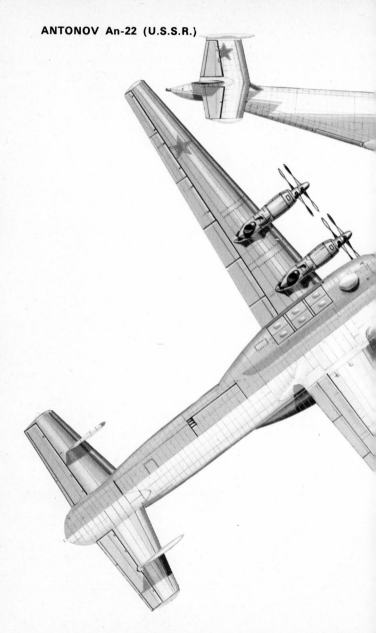

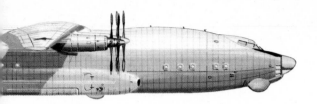

45

Antonov An-22 of the Soviet Air Force, 1970.
Engines: Four 15,000 s.h.p. Kuznetsov NK-12MA
turboprops. *Span:* 211 ft. 4 in. (64·40 m.). *Length:*
approx. 190 ft. 0 in. (57·91 m.). *Wing area:* 3,713·0
sq. ft. (345·00 sq. m.). *Maximum take-off weight:*
551,160 lb. (250,000 kg.). *Maximum speed:* 460
m.p.h. (740 km/hr.). *Range with payload of 99,200
lb. (45,000 kg.):* 6,800 miles (10,950 km.).

TUPOLEV Tu-95 (U.S.S.R.)

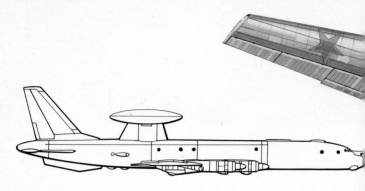

Tupolev 'Moss', airborne warning and control version of the Tu-114.

46

Tupolev Tu-95 Bear-B of the Soviet Air Force, *ca* 1963-64. *Engines:* Four 14,795 e.h.p. Kuznetsov NK-12MV turboprops. *Span:* 159 ft. 1½ in. (48·50 m.). *Length:* 155 ft. 10 in. (47·50 m.). *Wing area:* 3,153·8 sq. ft. (293·00 sq. m.). *Maximum take-off weight:* 341,745 lb. (155,000 kg.). *Maximum speed:* 500 m.p.h. (805 km/hr.) at 41,000 ft. (12,500 m.). *Maximum range with 24,250 lb. (11,000 kg.) weapons load:* 7,800 miles (12,550 km.). *All data estimated.*

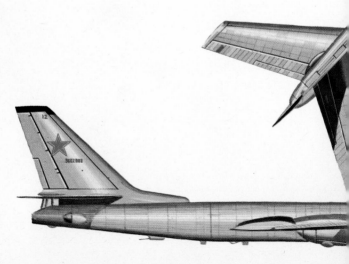

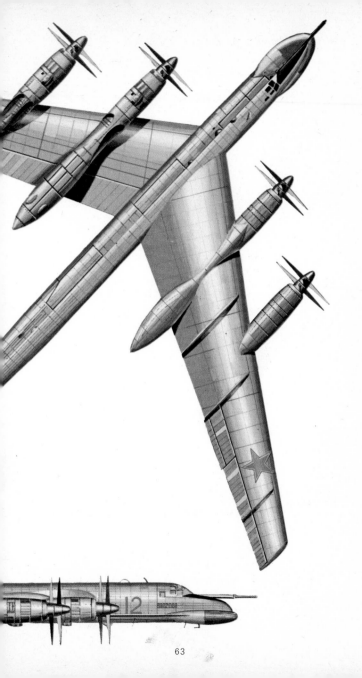

LOCKHEED U-2 (U.S.A.)

47

Lockheed WU-2A flown by Lockheed for the US Air Force Flight Dynamics
Laboratory, *ca* 1964. *Engine:* One 11,200 lb. (5,080 kg.) st Pratt & Whitney
J57-P-37A turbojet. *Span:* 80 ft. 0 in. (24·38 m.). *Length:* 49 ft. 7 in. (15·11
m.). *Wing area:* 565·0 sq. ft. (52·49 sq. m.). *Normal take-off weight:* 15,850
lb. (6,842 kg.). *Maximum speed:* 495 m.p.h. (797 km/hr.) at 40,000 ft. (12,200
m.). *Service ceiling:* 55,000 ft. (16,775 m.). *Range on internal fuel:* 2,200
miles (3,540 km.).

LOCKHEED SR-71 (U.S.A.)

48

Lockheed SR-71A of the 9th Strategic Reconnaissance Wing, USAF, Beale AFB (California), as displayed at SBAC's Farnborough International Air Show, September 1974. *Engines:* Two approx. 23,000/32,500 lb. (10,430/14,740 kg.) st Pratt & Whitney J58 (JT11D-20B) afterburning by-pass turbojets. *Span:* 55 ft. 7 in. (16·95 m.). *Length:* 107 ft. 5 in. (32·74 m.). *Height:* 18 ft. 6 in. (5·64 m.). *Maximum take-off weight:* approx. 170,000 lb. (77,110 kg.). *Maximum speed:* approx. 2,300 m.p.h. (3,700 km/hr.) at 80,000 ft. (24,400 m.). *Service ceiling:* over 80,000 ft. (24,400 m.). *Range without refuelling:* approx. 2,980 miles (4,800 km.).

49

Douglas A-4C (A4D-2N) Skyhawk of US Navy Squadron VA-153, USS *Constellation, ca* 1962. *Engine:* One 7,700 lb. (3,493 kg.) s.t. Wright J65-W-16A turbojet. *Span:* 27 ft. 6 in. (8·38 m.). *Length (incl probe):* 42 ft. 10¾ in. (13·07 m.). *Wing area:* 260·0 sq. ft. (24·16 sq. m.). *Normal take-off weight:* 17,295 lb. (7,845 kg.). *Maximum speed:* 680 m.p.h. (1,094 km/hr.) at sea level. *Maximum range on internal fuel:* 1,150 miles (1,850 km.).

50

McDonnell Douglas TA-4J Skyhawk of US Marine Corps Squadron VMT-103, *ca* 1971. *Engine:* One 8,500 lb. (3,855 kg.) s.t. Pratt & Whitney J52-P-6 turbojet. *Span and Wing area:* As for A-4C. *Length (excl probe):* 42 ft. 7¼ in. (12·98 m.). *Normal take-off weight:* approx. 22,500 lb. (10,206 kg.). *Maximum speed:* 675 m.p.h. (1,086 km/hr.) at sea level.

51

McDonnell Douglas A-4K Skyhawk of No. 75 Squadron, Royal New Zealand Air Force, 1971. *Engine:* One 9,300 lb. (4,218 kg.) s.t. Pratt & Whitney J52-P-8A turbojet. *Span and Wing area:* As for A-4C. *Length (excl probe):* 40 ft. 3¼ in. (12·27 m.). *Normal take-off weight:* 24,500 lb. (11,113 kg.). *Maximum speed with 4,000 lb. (1,814 kg.) weapon load:* 593 m.p.h. (954 km/hr.) at sea level. *Typical range with 4,000 lb. (1,814 kg.) weapon load:* 700 miles (1,125 km.).

BUCCANEER (U.K.)

52

Hawker Siddeley Buccaneer S.Mk 2A of No. 15 Squadron RAF, 1972. *Engines:* Two 11,100 lb. (5,035 kg.) st Rolls-Royce RB.168-1A Spey Mk 101 turbofans. *Span:* 44 ft. 0 in. (13·41 m.); *folded:* 19 ft. 11 in. (6·07 m.). *Length:* 63 ft. 5 in. (19·33 m.). *Wing area:* 514·7 sq. ft. (47·82 sq. m.). *Maximum take-off weight:* 62,000 lb. (28,123 kg.). *Maximum speed:* 645 m.p.h. (1,038 km/hr.) at 200 ft. (61 m.). *Typical operational range:* 2,300 miles (3,700 km.).

53

Grumman A-6A Intruder of US Navy Squadron VA-85, USS *America*, south-west Pacific area, *ca* 1968. *Engines:* Two 9,300 lb. (4,218 kg.) st Pratt & Whitney J52-P-8A turbojets. *Span:* 53 ft. 0 in. (16·15 m.). *Length:* 54 ft. 7 in. (16·64 m.). *Wing area:* 529·0 sq. ft. (49·15 sq. m.). *Maximum take-off weight:* 60,626 lb. (27,500 kg.). *Maximum speed:* 685 m.p.h. (1,102 km/hr.) at sea level. *Service ceiling:* 41,660 ft. (12,700 m.). *Typical combat range:* 1,920 miles (3,090 km.).

VIGILANTE (U.S.A.)

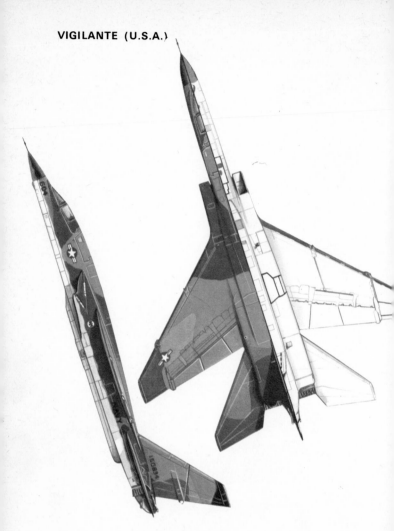

54

North American RA-5C Vigilante of US Navy Squadron RVAH-13, USS *Kitty Hawk* (CVA-63), southeast Asia, spring 1966. *Engines:* Two 11,870/17,860 lb. (5,385/8,101 kg.) st General Electric J79-GE-10 afterburning turbojets. *Span:* 53 ft. 0¼ in. (16·16 m.). *Length:* 75 ft. 10 in. (23·11 m.). *Wing area:* 769·0 sq. ft. (71·44 sq. m.). *Maximum take-off weight:* approx. 80,000 lb. (36,287 kg.). *Maximum speed:* 1,385 m.p.h. (2,230 km/hr.) at 40,000 ft. (12,200 m.). *Service ceiling:* 64,000 ft. (19,500 m.). *Maximum range on internal fuel:* 3,000 miles (4,830 km.).

55

Dassault Mirage IV-A of the Commandement des Forces Aériennes Stratégiques of the Armée de l'Air, *ca* 1965. *Engines:* Two 10,362/14,771 lb. (4,700/6,700 kg.) st SNECMA Atar 9K-50 afterburning turbojets. *Span:* 38 ft. 10½ in. (11·85 m.). *Length:* 77 ft. 1¼ in. (23·50 m.). *Wing area:* 839·6 sq. ft. (78·00 sq. m.). *Typical take-off weight:* 69,665 lb. (31,600 kg.). *Maximum speed:* 1,454 m.p.h. (2,340 km/hr.) at 36,000 ft. (11,000 m.). *Service ceiling:* 65,600 ft. (20,000 m.). *Maximum range with external tanks:* 2,485 miles (4,000 km.).

SKYWARRIOR (U.S.A.)

56

Douglas A-3B Skywarrior of US Navy Squadron VAH-6, *ca* 1962. *Engines:* Two 12,400 lb. (5,624 kg.) st Pratt & Whitney J57-P-10 turbojets. *Span:* 72 ft. 6 in. (22·10 m.). *Length:* 76 ft. 4 in. (23·27 m.). *Wing area:* 812·0 sq. ft. (75·43 sq. m.). *Normal take-off weight:* 73,000 lb. (33,112 kg.). *Maximum speed:* 610 m.p.h. (982 km/hr.) at 10,000 ft. (3,050 m.). *Service ceiling:* 41,000 ft. (12,500 m.). *Operational radius:* 1,050 miles (1,690 km.).

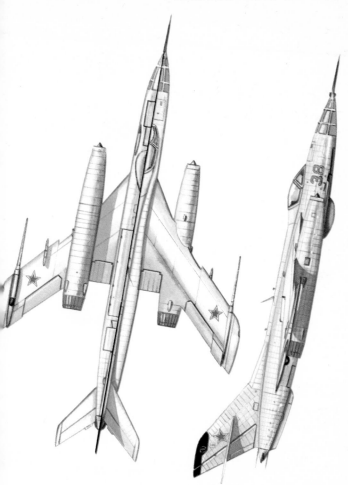

57

Yakovlev Yak-28 Brewer of the Soviet Air Force, *ca* 1963. *Engines:* Two 9,480/13,120 lb. (4,300/5,950 kg.) st. Tumansky RD-11 afterburning turbojets. *Span:* 42 ft. 6 in. (12·95 m.). *Length:* 71 ft. 0½ in. (21·65 m.). *Wing area:* 410·0 sq. ft. (38·00 sq. m.). *Maximum take-off weight:* 35,275 lb. (16,000 kg.). *Maximum speed:* 733 m.p.h. (1,180 km/hr.) at 36,000 ft. (11,000 m.). *Service ceiling:* 55,775 ft. (17,000 m.). *Maximum combat radius:* 575 miles (925 km.). *All data estimated.*

GENERAL DYNAMICS (MARTIN) RB-57F (U.S.A.)

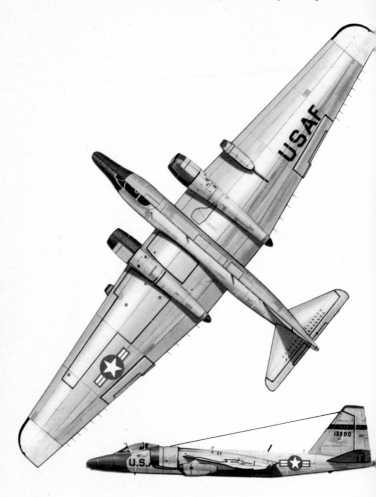

58

General Dynamics (Martin) RB-57F of the 58th Weather Reconnaissance Squadron, USAF, during 'Exercise Coldcat', Singapore, early 1969. *Engines:* Two 16,500 lb. (7,484 kg.) st Pratt & Whitney TF33-P-11A turbofans and two 2,900 lb. (1,315 kg.) st Pratt & Whitney J60-P-9 auxiliary turbojets. *Span:* 122 ft. 5 in. (37·32 m.). *Length:* 69 ft. 0 in. (21·03 m.). *Wing area:* 2,000·0 sq. ft. (185·8 sq. m.). *Maximum take-off weight:* 63,000 lb. (28,576 kg.). *Typical cruising speed:* 411 m.p.h. (661 km/hr.). *Service ceiling:* 60,800 ft. (18,500 m.). *Operational radius:* 1,475 miles (2,374 km.).

74

TUPOLEV Tu-16 (U.S.S.R.)

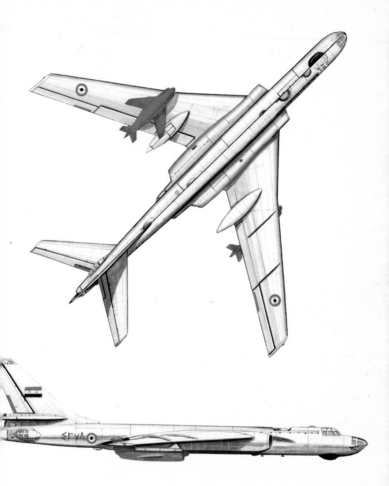

59

Tupolev Tu-16 Badger-A of the Egyptian Air Force, *ca* 1967. *Engines:* Two 20,950 lb. (9,500 kg.) st Mikulin AM-3M turbojets. *Span:* 110 ft. 0 in. (33·50 m.). *Length:* 120 ft. 0 in. (36·50 m.). *Wing area:* approx. 1,820·0 sq. ft. (169·00 sq. m.). *Normal take-off weight:* approx 150,000 lb. (68,000 kg.). *Maximum speed:* 587 m.p.h. (945 km/hr.) at 35,000 ft. (10,700 m.). *Service ceiling:* 42,650 ft. (13,000 m.). *Range with 6,614 lb. (3,000 kg.) bomb load:* 3,975 miles (6,400 km.).

75

TUPOLEV Tu-22 (U.S.S.R.)

60

Tupolev Tu-22 Blinder-A of the Soviet Air Force, *ca* 1968. *Engines:* Two
26,000 lb. (11,790 kg.) st afterburning turbojets of unknown type. *Span:*
90 ft. 10½ in. (27·70 m.). *Length:* 132 ft. 11½ in. (40·53 m.). *Wing area:*
2,045 sq. ft. (190·00 sq. m.). *Maximum take-off weight:* 184,970 lb. (83,900
kg.). *Maximum speed:* 920 m.p.h. (1,480 km/hr.) at 40,000 ft. (12,200 m.).
Service ceiling: 60,000 ft. (18,300 m.). *Maximum range:* 1,400 miles (2,250
km.). *All data estimated.*

TUPOLEV 'BACKFIRE' (U.S.S.R.)

61

Provisional illustration (see text) of a Tupolev 'Backfire-A' in Soviet Air Force insignia. *All data estimated. Engines:* Two 44,090 lb. (20,000 kg.) st (Kuznetsov?) afterburning turbofans. *Span (wings forward):* 105 ft. 0 in. (32·00 m.). *Span (wings swept):* 88 ft. 6 in. (27·00 m.). *Length:* 115 ft. 0 in. (35·00 m.). *Maximum take-off weight:* 273,375 lb. (124,000 kg.). *Maximum speed:* 1,485-1,650 m.p.h. (2,390-2,655 km/hr.) at 40,000 ft. (12,200 m.). *Maximum range on internal fuel:* 7,145 miles (11,500 km.).

VIKING (U.S.A.)

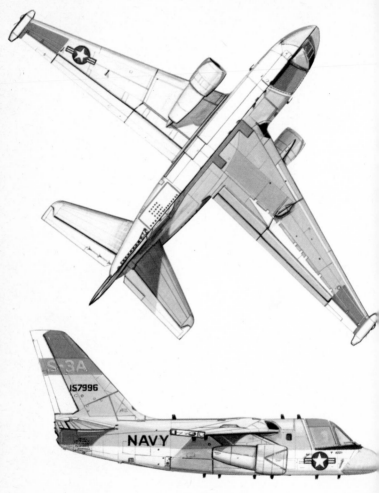

62

Lockheed S-3A Viking, fifth development aircraft for the US Navy, summer 1973. *Engines:* Two 9,275 lb. (4,207 kg.) st General Electric TF34-GE-2 turbofans. *Span:* 68 ft. 8 in. (20·93 m.). *Length:* 53 ft. 4 in. (16·26 m.). *Wing area:* 598·0 sq. ft. (55·56 sq. m.). *Normal take-off weight (ASW):* 42,500 lb. (19,277 kg.). *Maximum cruising speed:* over 403 m.p.h. (649 km/hr.). *Service ceiling:* over 35,000 ft. (10,670 m.). *Combat range:* more than 2,303 miles (3,705 km.).

63

Dassault Fan Jet Falcon (Mystère 20) of No. 412(T) Squadron, Canadian Armed Forces, 1968-69. *Engines:* Two 4,125 lb. (1,870 kg.) st General Electric CF700-2C turbofans. *Span:* 53 ft. 6 in. (16·30 m.). *Length:* 56 ft. 3 in. (17·15 m.). *Wing area:* 441·3 sq. ft. (41·00 sq. m.). *Maximum take-off weight:* 26,455 lb. (12,000 kg.). *Maximum cruising speed:* 534 m.p.h. (860 km/hr.) at 25,000 ft. (7,620 m.). *Absolute ceiling:* 42,000 ft. (12,800 m.). *Range with payload of 1,600 lb. (725 kg.):* 1,900 miles (3,050 km.).

KAWASAKI C-1 (Japan)

64

Kawasaki-built C-1, first pre-production aircraft in the insignia of the Japan Air Self-Defence Force, 1974. *Engines:* Two 14,500 lb. (6,575 kg.) st Pratt & Whitney JT8D-9 turbofans. *Span:* 100 ft. 4¾ in. (30·60 m.). *Length:* 95 ft. 1¾ in. (29·00 m.). *Wing area:* 1,297·0 sq. ft. (120·50 sq. m.). *Maximum take-off weight:* 85,320 lb. (38,700 kg.). *Maximum speed:* 501 m.p.h. (806 km/hr.) at 25,000 ft. (7,620 m.). *Service ceiling:* 38,000 ft. (11,580 m.). *Range with payload of 17,640 lb. (8,000 kg.):* 807 miles (1,300 km.).

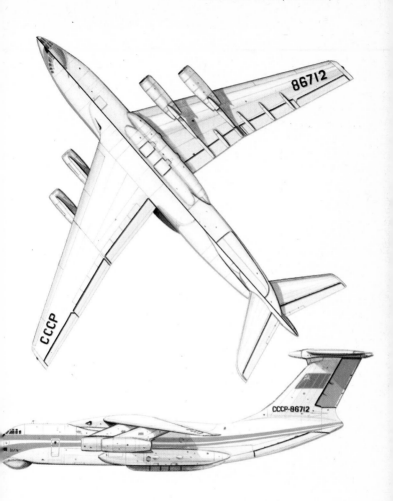

65

Ilyushin Il-76, second (?) prototype, as exhibited at Paris Air Show, May/June 1971. *Engines:* Four 26,455 lb. (12,000 kg.) st Soloviev D-30KP turbofans. *Span:* 165 ft. 8 in. (50·50 m.). *Length:* 152 ft. 10½ in. (46·59 m.). *Height:* 48 ft. 5 in. (14·76 m.). *Maximum take-off weight:* 346,125 lb. (157,000 kg.). *Cruising speed:* 528 m.p.h. (850 km/hr.) at 42,650 ft. (13,000 m.). *Range with maximum payload of 88,185 lb. (40,000 kg.):* 3,100 miles (5,000 km.).

BAC VC10 (U.K.)

66

BAC VC10 C. Mk 1 of No. 10 Squadron RAF Air Support Command, Brize
Norton, 1968. *Engines:* Four 21,800 lb. (9,888 kg.) st Rolls-Royce Conway
RCo.43 turbofans. *Span:* 146 ft. 2 in. (44·55 m.). *Length:* 158 ft. 8 in.
(48·36 m.). *Wing area:* 2,932·0 sq. ft. (272·40 sq. m.). *Maximum take-off
weight:* 323,000 lb. (146,510 kg.). *Maximum cruising speed:* 581 m.p.h.
(935 km/hr.) at 31,000 ft. (9,450 m.). *Service ceiling:* 42,000 ft. (12,800
m.). *Range with maximum payload of 57,400 lb. (26,030 kg.):* 3,900 miles
(6,275 km.).

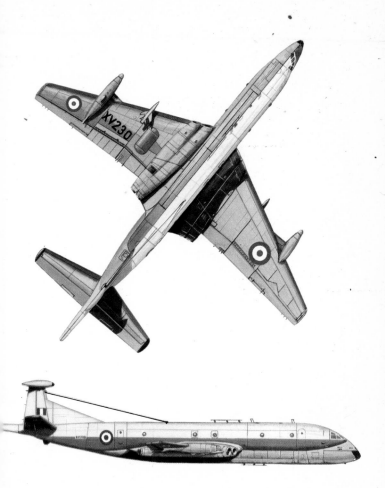

NIMROD (U.K.)

67

Hawker Siddeley Nimrod MR. Mk 1, first production aircraft, of No. 201 Squadron RAF Kinloss, 1970. *Engines:* Four 12,000 lb. (5,443 kg.) st Rolls-Royce RB.168 Spey Mk 250 turbofans. *Span:* 114 ft. 10 in. (35·00 m.). *Length:* 126 ft. 9 in. (38·63 m.). *Wing area:* 2,121·0 sq. ft. (197·00 sq. m.). *Typical take-off weight:* 175,500 lb. (79,605 kg.). *Maximum cruising speed:* 575 m.p.h. (926 km/hr.). *Typical endurance:* 12 hours.

VULCAN (U.K.)

68

Hawker Siddeley Vulcan B. Mk 2 of No. 35 Squadron, Tengah (Singapore), 1967. *Engines:* Four 20,000 lb. (9,072 kg.) st Rolls-Royce Bristol Olympus 301 turbojets. *Span:* 111 ft. 0 in. (33·83 m.). *Length:* 99 ft. 11 in. (30·45 m.). *Wing area:* 3,964·0 sq. ft. (368·27 sq. m.). *Maximum take-off weight:* approx 190,000 lb. (86,180 kg.). *Maximum speed:* 645 m.p.h. (1,038 km/hr.) at 40,000 ft. (12,200 m.). *Service ceiling:* 65,000 ft. (19,800 m.). *Low-level radius on internal fuel:* 1,725 miles (2,775 km.).

VICTOR (U.K.)

69

Handley Page Victor B. Mk 2R of No. 139 Squadron, RAF Bomber Command, 1966. *Engines:* Four 20,600 lb. (9,344 kg.) st Rolls-Royce Conway RCo.17 Mk 201 turbofans. *Span:* 120 ft. 0 in. (36·58 m.). *Length:* 114 ft. 11 in. (35·03 m.). *Wing area:* 2,597·0 sq. ft. (240·27 sq. m.). *Maximum take-off weight:* 223,000 lb. (101,153 kg.). *Maximum speed:* approx 650 m.p.h. (1,046 km/hr.) at 40,000 ft. (12,200 m.). *Service ceiling:* approx 60,000 ft. (18,300 m.). *Maximum unrefuelled range:* approx 2,300 miles (3,700 km.).

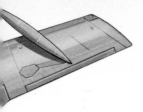

STRATOFORTRESS (U.S.A.)

70

Boeing B-52G Stratofortress of the 93rd Bomb Wing, USAF, 1968. *Engines:* Eight 13,750 lb. (6,237 kg.) st Pratt & Whitney J57-P-43W turbojets. *Span:* 185 ft. 0 in. (56·39 m.). *Length:* 157 ft. 7 in. (48·03 m.). *Wing area:* 4,000·0 sq. ft. (371·61 sq. m.). *Maximum take-off weight:* 480,000 lb. (217,720 kg.). *Maximum speed:* 630 m.p.h. (1,014 km/hr.) at 40,000 ft. (12,200 m.). *Service ceiling:* 55,000 ft. (16,750 m.). *Range with maximum internal bomb load:* 8,000 miles (12,875 km.).

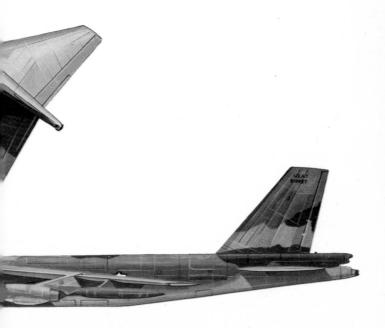

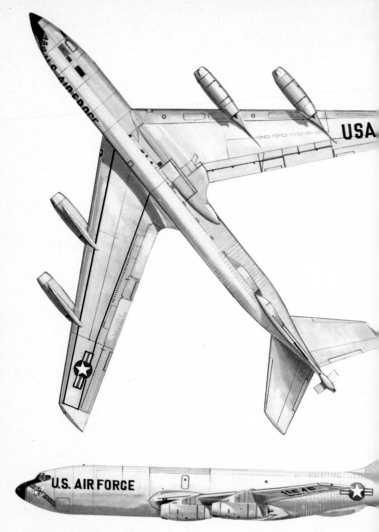

71

Boeing KC-135A of the 93rd Air Refueling Squadron, USAF Strategic Air Command, Castle AFB, California, *ca* spring 1957. *Engines:* Four 13,750 lb. (6,237 kg.) st Pratt & Whitney J57-P-59W turbojets. *Span:* 130 ft. 10 in. (39·88 m.). *Length:* 136 ft. 3 in. (41·53 m.). *Wing area:* 2,433·0 sq. ft. (226·04 sq. m.). *Maximum take-off weight:* 297,000 lb. (134,717 kg.). *Maximum cruising speed:* 530 m.p.h. (853 km/hr.) at 30,000 ft. (9,145 m.). *Service ceiling:* 50,000 ft. (15,240 m.). *Range with 120,000 lb. (54,430 kg.) of transferable fuel:* 1,150 miles (1,850 km.).

STRATOTANKER/STRATOLIFTER/BOEING E-3A (U.S.A.)

72

Boeing C-135B of Military Airlift Command, USAF, *ca* 1966. *Engines:* Four 18,000 lb. (8,165 kg.) st Pratt & Whitney TF33-P-5 turbofans. *Span and Wing area:* As for KC-135A. *Length:* 134 ft. 6 in. (41·00 m.). *Normal take-off weight:* 275,500 lb. (122,700 kg.). *Maximum cruising speed:* 604 m.p.h. (972 km/hr.) at 40,000 ft. (12,200 m.). *Service ceiling:* 45,000 ft. (13,725 m.). *Range with payload of 54,000 lb. (24,495 kg.):* 4,625 miles (7,445 km.).

73

Boeing EC-137D (second prototype for E-3A), 1973. *Engines:* Four 19,000 lb. (8,618 kg.) st Pratt & Whitney JT3D-7 turbofans.· *Span:* 145 ft. 9 in. (44·42 m.). *Length:* 152 ft. 11 in. (46·61 m.). *Wing area:* 3,050·0 sq. ft. (283·36 sq. m.). *Maximum take-off weight:* approx. 330,000 lb. (149,690 kg.). *Maximum cruising speed:* approx. 605 m.p.h. (973 km/hr.) at 25,000 ft. (7,620 m.). *Service ceiling:* approx. 39,000 ft. (11,885 m.). *Range/endurance:* 7-hour patrol at 1,150 miles (1,850 km.) from base.

MYASISHCHEV Mya-4 (U.S.S.R.)

74

Myasishchev 201-M (modified Bison-C) as exhibited at Domodedovo, 1967. *Engines:* Four 28,660 lb. (13,000 kg.) st Type D-15 turbojets. *Span:* 170 ft. 7¼ in. (52·00 m.). *Length:* 170 ft. 7¼ in. (52·00 m.). *Wing area:* approx. 3,229·17 sq. ft. (300·00 sq. m.). *Maximum take-off weight:* 363,760 lb. (165,000 kg.). *Maximum speed:* 621 m.p.h. (1,000 km/hr.) at 36,000 ft. (11,000 m.). *Service ceiling:* 51,180 ft. (15,600 m.). *Typical range:* 3,100 miles (5,000 km.).

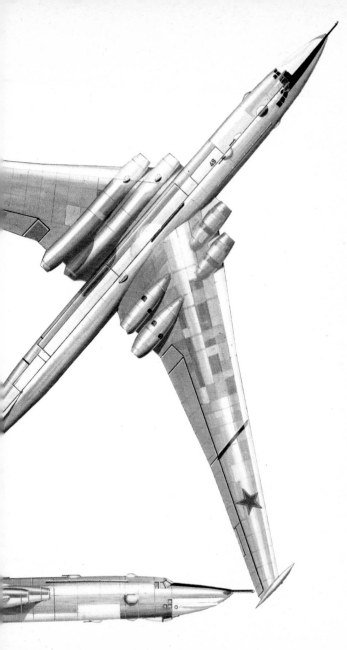

STARLIFTER (U.S.A.)

75

Lockheed C-141A StarLifter of the 437th Military Air Wing, USAF, *ca* 1967.
Engines: Four 21,000 lb. (9,525 kg.) st Pratt & Whitney TF33-P-7 turbofans.
Span: 159 ft. 11 in. (48·74 m.). *Length:* 145 ft. 0 in. (44·20 m.). *Wing
area:* 3,228·0 sq. ft. (299·9 sq. m.). *Maximum take-off weight:* 316,600 lb.
(143,600 kg.). *Maximum cruising speed:* 564 m.p.h. (908 km/hr.) at 24,250
ft. (7,400 m.). *Service ceiling:* 41,600 ft. (12,680 m.). *Range with maximum
payload of 70,847 lb. (32,136 kg.):* 4,080 miles (6,565 km.).

76

Lockheed C-5A Galaxy prototype in the insignia of Military Airlift Command,
USAF, 1969. *Data apply to production version. Engines:* Four 41,000 lb.
(18,600 kg.) st General Electric TF39-GE-1 turbofans. *Span:* 222 ft. 8½ in.
(67·88 m.). *Length:* 247 ft. 10 in. (75·54 m.). *Wing area:* 6,200 sq. ft. (576·00
sq. m.). *Maximum take-off weight:* 769,000 lb. (348,810 kg.). *Typical cruising
speed:* 518 m.p.h. (834 km/hr.). *Service ceiling:* 34,000 ft. (10,360 m.).
Range with payload of 220,967 lb. (100,228 kg.): 3,749 miles (6,033 km.).

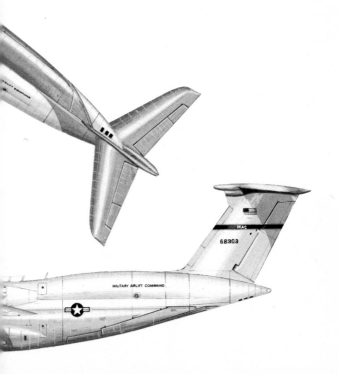

HUSTLER (U.S.A.)

77

General Dynamics (Convair) B-58A Hustler of the Flight Test Center, Systems Command, USAF, *ca* 1964, *Engines:* Four 10,000/15,600 lb. (4,536/7,076 kg.) st General Electric J79-GE-5B afterburning turbojets. *Span:* 56 ft. 10 in. (17·32 m.). *Length:* 96 ft. 9 in. (29·49 m.). *Wing area:* 1,542·0 sq. ft. (143·25 sq. m.). *Maximum take-off weight:* 164,500 lb. (74,616 kg.). *Maximum speed:* 1,385 m.p.h. (2,230 km/hr.) at 44,000 ft. (13,400 m.). *Service ceiling:* 60,000 ft. (18,300 m.). *Typical combat radius:* 1,200 miles (1,930 km.).

1 Antonov An-2 ('Colt')

The choice of a biplane configuration has many advantages for the range of duties that the An-2 has been required to perform during its long and varied career. The large wing area within a short span contributes to good STOL characteristics and good slow-speed handling, both eminently desirable in an aeroplane intended for use from small unprepared airstrips. The An-2 was originally designed, under the designation SKh-1 (Selskokhozyaistvenny = Agricultural Economic), to replace the veteran Po-2 biplane for such operations as crop-spraying and pest control. The prototype, powered by a 760 hp Shvetsov ASh-21 radial engine, was flown for the first time on 31 August 1947. This engine was retained in the first few production aircraft, but almost all An-2s built subsequently have had the 1,000 hp ASh-62IR. Soviet production, which began in 1948, had exceeded five thousand by 1960; since then the An-2 production centre has been the WSK factory at Mielec in Poland. The An-2 was also built in substantial quantities in the Chinese People's Republic. The standard personnel transport version, for both civil and military use, is the An-2P, which can accommodate 10–14 persons. Other variants include the agricultural An-2S (An-2R in Poland), the An-2ZA for high-altitude weather research, the An-2L water-bomber, and twin-float An-2V (An-2M in Poland). A modified agricultural version with enlarged vertical tail surfaces, the An-2M, was built in

limited numbers in the USSR. The civil versions are described in the *Private, Business and General Purpose Aircraft since 1946* volume in this series; in military service, the An-2P is employed extensively by the A-VDV arm of the Soviet Air Force as a light passenger or freight transport (Polish designations of this version are An-2T and An-2TP), ambulance aircraft (Polish designation An-2S), radio and navigation trainer, and glider tug. Many, like the example illustrated, are used by the DOSAAF for parachute training. Polish designation of this version is An-2TD. Outside of the Soviet Union, military An-2s have also been supplied to the air arms of Afghanistan, Albania, Bulgaria, Cambodia, Cuba, Czechoslovakia, Egypt, the German Democratic Republic, Hungary, Iraq, the Korean Democratic People's Republic, Mali, Mongolia, Romania, Syria, Tanzania, North Vietnam, the Yemen and Yugoslavia. Some An-2s have given way to a later Antonov design, the An-14 monoplane, but such replacement has not been widespread, and the older type continues in large-scale service.

2 Neiva Regente

Built by the Sociedade Construtora Aeronáutica Neiva Ltda of São José dos Campos, the Regente bears a broad superficial resemblance to the Cessna Model 150 and is used by the Fôrça Aérea Brasileira as a 4-seat utility and AOP aircraft. The civil-registered first prototype (PP-ZTP) was flown on 7 September 1961, and was designated Model 360C by the manufacturer. This was placed in production as the U-42 (later C-42) for the Brazilian Air Force, for whom a total of eighty were built with 180 hp Continental O-360-A1D flat-four engines. The first production C-42 Regente was flown in February 1965, and delivery of the initial production version was completed by the end of 1968. Meanwhile, in January 1967 Neiva had flown the YL-42 prototype (3120), intended to replace the Brazilian Air Force's L-6 Paulistinha and Cessna O-1 Bird Dog lightplanes in the AOP, liaison and observation roles. This differed from the C-42 chiefly in having a Continental IO-360-D flat-six engine and a cut-down rear fuselage, with glazing at the rear of the 3-seat cabin to improve the all-round view. Manufacturer's designation of the L-42 is Model 420L. Forty production L-42s were ordered for the Brazilian Air Force, the first of them flying in June 1969 and the last being delivered in March 1971. Provision is made in this version for four underwing attachments for light bombs, rockets or other stores.

3 Helio Super Courier

The Super Courier can trace its ancestry back to the 2-seat, 65 hp Helioplane, first flown on 8 April 1949 and itself based on the Piper Vagabond. The idea behind the design was to produce a lightplane with particularly good STOL and low-speed handling qualities, and from the original Helioplane evolved

by Dr Otto Koppen and Mr Lynn Bollinger were subsequently developed a succession of later models which included the H-391 Courier (first flown 1952), H-392 Strato-Courier (1957) and H-395 Super Courier. The last-named was a 4/5-seat aircraft, and was first flown in 1958. Later that year three Super Couriers were evaluated by the USAF under the designation L-28A. In 1962, when the US adopted a new designation system common to all three services, these became known as U-10As, and an additional quantity was ordered for 'special military duties' with Strategic and Tactical Air Commands. In the following year orders were placed by the US Army (twenty) and the Air National Guard (twenty-four). The standard USAF version is still the U-10A, but later versions are the U-10B and U-10D. Both have greater range than the U-10A; the U-10B, fitted with paratroop doors, has a maximum endurance of more than 10 hours, and the U-10D can seat six passengers in addition to the pilot. Super Courier operations in Southeast Asia included leaflet-dropping, sky-shouting and other psychological warfare activities, and the dropping of medical supplies and comforts to beleaguered South Vietnamese communities.

4 Douglas A-1 Skyraider

The Skyraider may perhaps be said to have had greatness thrust upon it, for it was due for retirement after 5 years of service with the US Navy when the Korean war broke out in

1950. Its record during the next 3 years' conflict, and its amazing versatility, combined to keep it in continued production until 1957 when, after a 12-year run, the Douglas factories had turned out three thousand one hundred and eighty Skyraiders. Rather more than half of these were accounted for by the first five models (including one thousand and fifty-one A-1Ds), which had passed out of front-line service by the mid-1960s; the remainder comprised six hundred and seventy A-1Es, seven hundred and thirteen A-1Hs, and seventy-two A-1Js. The A-1E was primarily a 2-seat attack bomber, but capable of being converted by a ready-made kit system to night attack, early warning, ECM (EA-1E), 12-seat transport, 4-litter ambulance, 2,000 lb (907 kg) freighter, photographic reconnaissance or target towing duties. The A-1H is a single-seat low-altitude attack bomber, the A-1J being similar except for a higher-powered engine and an airframe strengthened to carry a tremendous variety of loads. The Skyraider's load-carrying capacity is one of its most remarkable features, and has played a major part in the success of this aeroplane under operational conditions. The specification to which it was designed called for a load of 1,000 lb (454 kg), but Skyraiders have flown regularly with more than 8,000 lb (3,630 kg) of external ordnance, and the type has been flown with more than 14,000 lb (6,350 kg) of underwing stores – greater than the aeroplane's own basic empty weight.

The Skyraider's variety of load is equally impressive, and is augmented by four 20 mm wing cannon. Skyraiders had been withdrawn from US Navy service by the end of 1967, but even in the early 1970s the USAF still operated several squadrons in Vietnam, and the South Vietnamese Air Force has received more than a hundred A-1Es and A-1Hs. Other Skyraiders in the Far East at that time included about a dozen A-1Ds, which were resold by France in 1965 to the air force of Cambodia. Ex-French A-1Ds have also been supplied to the Republic of Chad (five) and the Central African Republic (ten).

5 Breguet Alizé (Tradewind)

To pack all the radar and electronic gear for finding the modern submarine, and the weapons to attack it, into a modest-sized airframe, and still leave room for the engine, a 3-man crew and normal carrier equipment, is no easy task, yet it was done in the Alizé without resorting to a large, fixed external radome such as is employed in many larger aircraft. The Alizé was derived from the mixed-powerplant Vultur strike aircraft designed in 1948, although the first true Alizé prototype did not fly until 6 October 1956. A second prototype and three pre-production Alizés were followed by seventy-five production aircraft for the Aéronavale, the first of which was flown on 26 March 1959, and twelve for the Indian Navy. The latter, delivered in 1961, serve with 310 Squadron aboard the carrier *Vikrant,* while those in French service (since 1959) equipped Flottilles 4F, 6F and 9F. About thirty Alizés remained in service at the end of 1972, with Flottille 4F (aboard the *Foch* and *Clémenceau*) and the shore-based Flottille 6F. They are being gradually replaced by SA 321G Super Frelon helicopters for the ASW role. The Alizé's CSF search radar is in a retractable 'dustbin' housing. Aft of this is the internal weapons bay, which has space for a homing torpedo or three 160 kg depth charges; and two similar or 175 kg charges, two Nord AS.12 or AS.11 missiles, or six 5 in aerial rockets, can be suspended underwing. The large 'knuckle' fairings on the wing leading edges house the retracted main landing gear; endurance of the Alizé is $3\frac{1}{2}$ to 4 hours.

6 Westland (Fairey) Gannet

The first Gannets, the anti-submarine Mk 1s, began to serve with the Fleet Air Arm in 1955, and were joined in the following year by the more powerful AS. Mk 4, total production of these two versions being two hundred and fifty-six. Corresponding versions for ASW and radar observer training were the T.2 and T.5 (thirty-eight and eight built respectively), and with modifications to incorporate more advanced electronics, some AS.4s were redesignated AS.6 and AS.7. The Gannet no longer serves in these roles. On 20 August 1958, there took place the first flight of a much-redesigned Gannet, the AEW.

Mk 3 all-weather early warning aircraft. Carrying a pilot and two radar operators, the Gannet 3 had an entirely new fuselage, an APS-20 search radar in an enormous 'guppy' radome under the belly, a more powerful Mamba engine, enlarged vertical tail surfaces and provision for underwing drop-tanks. Forty-four Mk 3s were built, the first production example being flown on 2 December 1958. These aircraft were delivered to No. 849 Squadron (whose motto, appropriately, is *Primus Video* – 'I see first'), which is now based at RAF Lossiemouth in Scotland. This squadron also operates five Gannet COD. Mk 4s, converted from AS.4s for carrier on-board delivery duties on behalf of HMS *Ark Royal.* A feature of all marks of the Gannet, unique among service aircraft, is the Double Mamba turboprop engine. Fundamentally, this comprises two engines each driving a separate propeller shaft, one turning inside the other; either engine can be shut down while the other is used for cruising. This gives the aircraft – particularly when auxiliary drop-tanks are carried – an extremely useful patrol radius from its base. Overall Gannet production amounted to three prototypes and three hundred and forty-six production aircraft, of which Australia received forty-two, Germany sixteen and Indonesia eighteen.

7 Cessna O-2

Cessna's first CLT (centre-line thrust) aircraft to fly was the Model 336 Skymaster, which made its first flight on 28 February 1961. Between then and January 1965, one hundred and ninety-five Skymasters were built before giving way to the much-improved Model 337 Super Skymaster with restyled rear nacelle, fully-retractable landing gear and considerably superior performance. One of the attractions of the Model 337 (see the *Private Aircraft* volume in this series) is its low operating noise level, and this was no doubt a factor in the USAF decision of 1966 to replace its O-1 Bird Dog FAC (Forward Air Controller) aircraft by the later Cessna type. The initial military version, designated O-2A, seats up to 6 people, has full dual controls and is fitted with four underwing attachments for gun pods, rocket launchers, photo-flares or other stores. Two hundred and ninety-nine O-2As were ordered by the USAF, and twelve were supplied in 1970 to the Imperial Iranian Air Force for liaison, observation and training. A psychological warfare version, designated O-2B, is basically similar but carries advanced systems for communications, air-to-ground broadcasting and leaflet dropping. Thirty-one were produced initially for the USAF by converting commercial Model 337s, delivery of these beginning in March 1967; by December 1970 a combined total of five hundred and ten O-2A/O-2Bs had been delivered. 'Off the shelf' commercial Cessna 337s have been supplied in small numbers to the Ecuadorean Air Force and the Venezuelan Navy. Reims Aviation in France,

which licence-builds and markets the commercial 337, flew on 26 May 1970 the prototype of a military STOL version known as the FTMA-Milirole, fitted with larger-area flaps; but no production of this version was undertaken.

8 Britten-Norman BN-2A Islander and Defender

First flown on 13 June 1965, the 10-seat Britten-Norman Islander has since become one of the world's most successful and popular third-level and commuter transport aircraft, with more than six hundred examples sold by mid-1974. The Islander and its three-engined derivative, the Trislander, are fully described in the *Airliners since 1946* volume in this series. In 1971 Britten-Norman first revealed a new version, known as the Defender. With local strengthening of the airframe and other minimal changes, this is otherwise similar to the standard BN-2A, and can be employed for a variety of tasks including personnel transport, communications, liaison and patrol or 'policing' duties. Islanders/Defenders have been sold to the Abu Dhabi Defence Force (four), British Army Parachute Association, Ghana Air Force (eight), Guyana Defence Force (three), Royal Hong Kong Auxiliary Air Force (one), Jamaica Defence Force (one), Malagasy Air Force (one), Mexican Air Force (three), Sultan of Oman's Air Force (eight) and Turkish Air Force (two). The Defender can be utilised as a light attack aircraft, with four underwing pylons carrying a maximum 2,300 lb (1,043 kg) external load of gun or rocket pods, photo-flares, bombs or auxiliary fuel tanks. Two pairs of beam-firing 7·62 mm machine-guns can be mounted in the cabin. A 30 mile (48 km) range nose-mounted weather radar is optional, permitting the Defender to take advantage of its 10-hour endurance to conduct search and rescue missions, and the internal layout can be modified for para-dropping, ambulance or aerial survey use.

9 Piaggio P.166

Existence of the Piaggio P.166 twin-engined feeder-line/executive transport was first announced in March 1957, and the prototype (I-RAIF) made its first flight on 26 November of that year. Basically, the design represented a scaling-up of the Italian company's P.136 amphibian, retaining the latter's gull wing configuration combined with an enlarged landplane fuselage instead of the flying-boat hull. The P.166's civilian career is described in the *Private Aircraft* volume; fifty-one were built as P.166Ms for the Aeronautica Militare Italiano. The AMI P.166Ms are used for light tactical transport, communications, ambulance work and training. The AMI received, in 1972–73, the first of twenty P.166S, a search and surveillance version with nose radar which had flown for the first time in October 1968. Nine of this version were also supplied to No. 27 Squadron of the South African Air Force, which ordered a second batch of nine in 1973. The SAAF aircraft

are known by the name Albatross, and are used for coastal and fishery patrol.

10 Mitsubishi MU-2

Design work on the MU-2, Mitsubishi's first entry into the executive/feederliner market, began in 1959, and the first of three flying prototypes (JA 8620) made its maiden flight on 14 September 1963 powered by two 562 shp Turboméca Astazou IIK turboprop engines. Initial production version, from 1965, was the AiResearch-engined MU-2B, and since then a succession of different models have appeared of which the latest, up to late 1974, was the MU-2M. Total orders for all MU-2 versions had by then reached well over three hundred and fifty, of which forty were for the Japanese armed forces: ten MU-2Cs for the Ground Self-Defence Force; and sixteen MU-2Es, six MU-2Js and eight MU-2Ks for the Air Self-Defence Force. The MU-2C, which has the JGSDF designation LR-1, was first flown on 11 May 1967, with delivery beginning at the end of the following month. It is basically similar to the commercial MU-2B, but with an unpressurised fuselage and (on one aircraft) an extra fuselage fuel tank instead of wing-tip tanks. The LR-1s are used for liaison and reconnaissance/support duties, aircraft for the latter role having provision for a pair of 13 mm nose machine-guns, a light load of bombs or rockets, and either reconnaissance cameras or sideways-looking radar. The MU-2E is an unpressurised search and rescue version distinguishable by its 'thimble' nose radome, bulged rear observation windows, and a sliding port-side door for lifeboat-dropping. It first flew on 15 August 1967. The MU-2J (for flight calibration duties) and MU-2K (rescue) versions both have more powerful 724 ehp TPE 331-6-251M turboprops; the MU-2K can be distinguished by fuselage external fairings which house the main landing gear when retracted. Six MU-2Fs are operated on target towing duties on behalf of the Swedish Air Force; the Mexican Air Force operates an MU-2J as a VIP transport, and two others for similar duties were delivered to the government of Zaïre.

11 Beagle Basset

When the Beagle company was formed in 1960, most of its early offerings were revisions or adaptations of earlier Auster designs. The first entirely new design to appear was the Beagle B.206X, which flew for the first time on 15 August 1961, powered by two 260 hp Continental IO-470-A engines, and from this was developed the slightly larger Basset CC.Mk 1 for the RAF. The Ministry of Aviation ordered two pre-production aeroplanes, with more powerful GIO-470 engines, which Beagle designated B.206Z1 and Z2, and the second of these became the Basset prototype XS743, making its maiden flight on 20 February 1964. Twenty production B.206R Bassets (XS765–784) followed, for service with Nos. 26, 32 and 207 Squadrons, the first of these flying on 24 December 1964,

and the remainder being delivered during 1965. The Basset had a slightly larger rear door than the civil B.206 Series I, and seats for up to 8 people, including the pilot(s). These handsome little aeroplanes augmented, and eventually replaced, the RAF's Devons and few surviving Ansons on communications and light personnel transport duties. The Basset had been phased out of RAF service by the spring of 1974.

12 Beechcraft U-21

First of the post-war Beech 'twins' adopted by the US armed forces was the Twin-Bonanza, four of which were acquired by the US Army as YL-23s for evaluation in 1952. Subsequent contracts covered fifty-five L-23As, forty L-23Bs, eighty-five L-23Ds and six L-23Es, to which the name Seminole was applied. Most of the A and B models were later brought up to D standard, and in 1962 the L-23D and L-23E were redesignated U-8D and U-8E respectively. The U-8F (originally L-23F) was a developed version with a larger fuselage, and was based on the Model 65 Queen Air; three pre-series and sixty-eight production examples were completed for the US Army, and others were supplied to the Japan Maritime Self-Defence Force (twenty-nine) and the air forces of Uruguay and Venezuela (six).

On 22 June 1961 Beech flew the prototype of a new and improved Queen Air, the Model 65-80, with 380 hp IGSO-540-A1A engines and a sweptback fin and rudder; this in turn was superseded by the Model 65-A80, with a 5 ft 0 in (1·52 m) increase in wing span, enlarged nose section and higher gross weight. From the remodelled Queen Air was developed the military U-21, principally to provide the US Army with a new light transport and utility aircraft for use in Southeast Asia. A prototype was evaluated in 1963, and deliveries of the production U-21A (corresponding to the commercial Model 65-A90-1) began in May 1967. One hundred and twenty-four were ordered, followed by three U-21Bs and two U-21Cs; these all have 550 shp PT6A-20 engines. Standard utility transport version is the U-21A, accommodating a crew of 2 and up to 10 passengers or 3 stretchers. The RU-21A and electronics reconnaissance RU-21D are 'special-purpose' models. With 620 shp PT6A-29 engines and a gross weight of 10,900 lb (4,944 kg) the aircraft is known as the RU-21B (= Model 65-A90-2) and RU-21C (= Model 65-A90-3); the RU-21E is an electronics reconnaissance version of the Model 65-A90-4, of which sixteen were ordered in 1970; the U-21F, of which five were ordered in 1971 together with seventeen RU-21Fs, corresponds to the pressurised King Air A100. Three Super King Air 200s for the US Army, for electronics reconnaissance, are designated RU-21J. Standard King Air C90s have been ordered by the USAF (one VC-6B), JMSDF (one) and Spanish Air Ministry (six); and King Air A100s by the Royal Moroccan Air Force (six) and Spanish Air Ministry (two).

13 Shorts Skyvan

The SC.7 Skyvan was the first product of Shorts' newly-formed Light Aircraft Division, and was begun as a private venture in early 1959. It was originally conceived as a piston-engined cargo and livestock transport, and the first prototype (G-ASCN), powered by two 390 hp Continental GTSIO-520 engines, flew for the first time on 17 January 1963. The piston-engined version was later dropped in favour of the Skyvan Series 2, the same aircraft acting also as the prototype for this version (first flight 2 October 1963) after refitting with 520 shp Turboméca Astazou II turboprops. In the event, however, the major production version was to be the Series 3, which adopted the Canadian TPE 331 engine as standard, and the few Series 2s built were later converted to Series standard. The Skyvan is produced in two civil models, the Series 3 and 3A (the latter having a higher take-off weight), and the military Series 3M. The Skyvan 3M prototype (G-AXPT) flew for the first time in early 1970, about a year after the first order for this version had been received, from the Austrian Air Force, for two. Subsequent military customers for this versatile STOL transport have included the Argentine Naval Prefectura (five), Ecuador Army Air Force (one), Ghana Air Force (six), Indonesian Air Force (three, operated on behalf of the Ministry of the Interior), Royal

Nepalese Army (two), Sultan of Oman's Air Force (sixteen), Singapore Air Defence Command (six, including three for search and rescue, operated by No. 121 Squadron), Royal Thai Police Department (three) and Yemen Arab Republic Air Force (two). The Skyvan 3M is capable of a variety of duties, including assault transport (22 equipped troops); paratrooping (16 paratroops and a dispatcher); supply dropping; medical evacuation (12 stretchers and 2 attendants); vehicle or ordnance transport; or cargo transport (up to 5,200 lb; 2,358 kg of freight). For vehicle loading and unloading, a lightweight ramp is carried internally.

14 CASA 212 Aviocar

Although intended for both military and civil applications, it is in the former capacity that the C.212 Aviocar is being developed initially, primarily to replace the ageing CASA Azor and older transports in the Spanish Air Force inventory. Detail design began in 1966, the emphasis being placed on versatility and STOL performance. The first of two prototypes (XT.12-1) flew for the first time on 26 March 1971, powered by two 755 ehp AiResearch TPE 331-2-201 turboprop engines. The second prototype (first flight 23 October 1971) was similarly powered originally, but in early 1972 was refitted with the higher-powered TPE 331-5-251C version of this engine which is installed on the pre-production and production aircraft. Of twelve pre-production Aviocars, four are to be used by CASA for civil development; the remainder were to be completed as two navigation trainers and six for photographic survey duties. In the former, accommodation is provided for an instructor and five trainees; the photographic version carries two aerial cameras and a fully-equipped darkroom. The first pre-production Aviocar made its first flight on 17 November 1972. These twelve aircraft are being followed by thirty-two production aircraft for the Spanish Air Force, twenty-eight for the Portuguese Air Force, which has an option on a further twelve, and three for the Indonesian Air Force. Three of the Spanish Air Force batch are earmarked for navigation training duties, the remaining twenty-nine being intended for troop/freight transport duties under the designation T.12. In addition to the normal 2-man crew, these will have accommodation for 15 paratroops and an instructor or dispatcher; 10 stretchers and 3 sitting patients, or a maximum of 18 stretchers; or 2,000 kg (4,410 lb) of cargo, including small vehicles. Cargo loading is via a ramp/door in the underside of the rear fuselage, which is openable in flight and is fitted with small external wheels to permit the aircraft to manoeuvre on the ground with the door open.

15 CASA 207 Azor

The Azor was the third general transport to come from the modest-sized Spanish aircraft industry since the war. The small CASA 201 Alcotan, which served in both military and civil roles, was followed by the CASA 202 Halcon, and the Azor was, in essence, an enlarged version of the Halcon. It was intended originally for the civil market, gaining its C of A in January 1958, the prototype having flown for the first time on 28 September 1955. The Spanish government, however, decided to order an initial batch of ten for the Ejército del Aire, by whom they were designated T.7A. These aircraft carry a crew of 4 and up to 40 passengers, and began to enter service with the Aviación de Trasporte in 1960. Two were fitted with 2,400 hp Pratt & Whitney Double Wasp radial engines, but the Hercúles 730 was the standard powerplant. The Azor was intended to replace the CASA 352-L (Ju 52/3m), though the latter type remained in service for a time. A further ten Azors were subsequently ordered, these being designated T.7B and serving as freight transports. They can be distinguished from the T.7A version by the large cargo door at the rear of the fuselage.

16 Douglas C-47 Skytrain

Such has been the universal presence of the DC-3, in both military and commercial service, during and since World War 2 that one is apt to forget that it was already a major airliner by 1938, the prototype having flown for the first time in December 1935. Nearly forty years later it is still a workhorse of a considerable number of small airlines the world over, and serves with the air arms of more than fifty

nations, from Argentina to Yugoslavia. It would be near-impossible to estimate the total number still operating, but it probably amounts to a very substantial proportion of the nearly eleven thousand that were built in the USA. What is perhaps an even greater tribute to this supremely adaptable aeroplane is that more than a dozen variants were still actively employed by the United States' own forces in the late 1960s, including some employed in Vietnam as AC-47 ground attack aircraft. With three General Electric 7·62 mm Miniguns firing 18,000 rounds per minute from the portside doorways, the AC-47 was euphemistically referred to by its crews as 'Puff, the magic dragon', among other titles. In its basic transport configuration the C-47 nominally has accommodation for a 7,500 lb (3,400 kg) cargo load or 28 troops, but in wartime it is known to have successfully, if not comfortably, carried at least 74 men. A considerable number of Lisunov Li-2s (the Russian licence version) remain active with many pro-Soviet states. The so-called 'Super DC-3', with redesigned, square-cut wing and tail surfaces, uprated engines and other improvements, was built for service under C-117D series designations (formerly R4D-8). Ninety-eight were converted, for service with the US Navy and Marine Corps.

17 Fokker-VFW Troopship

The Fokker Friendship short- to medium-range passenger airliner has been the most successful turboprop-engined civil transport produced anywhere in the world. Since the flight of the first prototype on 24 November 1955, several hundreds have been built for airline and private customers, both by Fokker in Holland and by Fairchild in the United States. These are described in the *Airliners since 1946* volume in this series. The Philippine Air Force received one Mk 100 Friendship as a VIP transport, and three others went to the Netherlands' own air force. In addition to these, there is a specialised military version known as the Troopship, which differs from the airliner models in having a big cargo-loading door in the forward port side of the fuselage, an enlarged paratroop door on each side aft, and a reinforced floor to take military loads. Nine Mk 300 Troopships, together with the three Friendships already mentioned, were delivered to No. 334 Squadron of the Koninklijke Luchtmacht, two subsequently being converted as NASARR trainers. A maximum cargo load of 13,553 lb (6,148 kg) can be carried by the Mk 400M Troopship, and in less than 24 man-hours its internal layout can be converted from the cargo configuration to accommodate up to 45 paratroops, or 24 casualty stretchers plus seats for 9 orderlies or sitting patients. Sales of Mk 400M and Mk 600M Troopships (the latter does not have reinforced flooring) have subsequently been made to the air forces of Argentina (eight, plus four Friendships), Ghana (five, plus one Friendship),

Iran (twelve, plus six Friendships, to the Air Force; two, plus two Friendships, to the Navy; and two to the National Geographic Organisation), the Ivory Coast (one, plus one Friendship), Nigeria (four, plus two Friendships) and Sudan (four). The Mk 500 airliner is also available in Troopship form. In addition, two examples of the stretched FH-227B version, built by Fairchild, were supplied to the Uruguayan Ministry of Defence and three to the Mexican government.

18 FMA I.A.50 GII

Development of this multi-purpose military transport began in early 1960 when, after abandoning the earlier I.A.47 project for a 12/14-seat piston-engined feederliner, the Fabrica Militar de Aviones in Argentina began instead to study the possibilities of a turboprop-powered development of the I.A.35 Huanquero. The outcome of this was the prototype Guarani I (LQ-HER, originally known as Constancia II), which retained much of the basic Huanquero airframe but was given a lengthened fuselage and was powered by two 870 shp Turboméca Bastan IIIA turboprop engines. The twin-tailed Guarani I was flown for the first time on 6 February 1962, and designs were completed for both military transport and 10-seat executive transport versions. However, some 5 months earlier a third design had also been completed, this having 930 shp Bastan VI engines, a shortened rear fuselage and a single sweptback fin and rudder. This version, known as the I.A.50 Guarani II, first flew in prototype form (LV-X27) on 23 April 1963, followed by a second prototype (TX-01) and one pre-production machine. An initial batch of eighteen Guarani IIs was ordered, the first six of which were delivered to the Fuerza Aérea Argentina between May and December 1966. Fourteen of these eighteen (serial numbers T-111 to T-124) were allocated as troop transports to I Air Brigada at El Palomar; the other four comprised two equipped for aerial photography and survey work (F-31 and F-32), one VIP transport for the FAA (TX-110) and one staff transport (5-T-30) for the Aviación Naval. Four other Guarani IIs (the designation was altered to GII in 1970–71) were built for photographic duties with the Instituto Geográfico Militar, and one was completed as a Presidential transport. These twenty-three production aircraft were followed by a further fifteen, ordered in October 1969, which have a lightened structure and redesigned interiors. The standard military transport version can accommodate, in addition to the 2-man crew, up to 15 paratroops or 6 stretchers and 2 medical attendants.

19 EMBRAER EMB-110 Bandeirante

The first indigenous transport aircraft design to emerge from the expanding Brazilian aircraft industry, the Bandeirante (pioneer) originated as the IPD/PAR-6504, designed to a Ministry of Aeronautics specification by the PAR-Departamento de Aeronaves of the Centro Técnico Aeroespacial under the initial guidance of the French aircraft designer Max Holste. The first of three YC-95 prototypes (2130) made its first flight on 26 October 1968, followed by the second (2131) on 19 October 1969 and the third (PP-ZCN) on 26 June 1970. These aircraft were powered by 550 shp PT6A-20 turboprop engines and had circular cabin windows. The fourth Bandeirante, representative of the production version, had more powerful PT6A-27 engines, modified nose, flight deck and cabin window contours, an additional cabin window in each side and a lengthened fuselage, and was utilised for the structural test programme. The first of eighty C-95 Bandeirantes for the Brazilian Air Force was flown for the first time on 9 August 1972, and deliveries began in February 1973. About twenty more have been ordered by commercial operators, including Transbrasil (six) and VASP (eight). The Brazilian Air Force aircraft will replace the ageing fleet of Beechcraft C-45s. The Bandeirante carries a crew of 2, and the main cabin has accommodation for up to 15 passengers or four stretcher patients. The EMB-110B and EMB-110E are, respectively, aerial photography and executive transport versions. Proposed developments include the maritime patrol EMB-111, with a large nose-mounted search radar and PT6A-34 engines; and the pres-

urised EMB-120 transport, with
'T6A-45 turboprops, a prototype of
which was due to fly for the first time
in late 1975.

20 De Havilland Canada DHC-4 Caribou

De Havilland Canada's avowed
intent, in designing the Caribou,
was to bridge the gap between the
helicopter and the conventional
transport, producing an aeroplane
combining the payload of the latter
with a first-class STOL airfield
performance. Its success in achiev-
ing this objective has been borne
out by the experience, under operational conditions, of the Caribou's
extended use by the UNEF in the
Mediterranean, Middle East and
Congo, and by the US and Australian forces in Vietnam. The
Caribou, which flew for the first
time on 30 July 1958, is able to
transport 32 armed troops or 26
paratroops. Other cargoes may
include 2 loaded jeeps, 1 howitzer
or 3 tons of freight. For casualty
evacuation, the Caribou can take
22 stretchers and up to 8 other
passengers, either sitting patients
or medical attendants. Its excellent
STOL characteristics, which make
it independent of prepared airstrips,
enable it to operate in either jungle
or desert terrain, a factor amply
supported by the sources of the
orders for three hundred and seven
aircraft which were subsequently
placed, nearly all for military versions. These have come from the US
Army (one hundred and fifty-nine),
and from the armed forces or
governments of Abu Dhabi (five),

Australia (thirty-one), Cameroun
(two), Canada (nine CC-108),
Ghana (eight), India (twenty),
Kenya (six), Kuwait (two), Malaysia (sixteen), Muscat and Oman
(three), Spain (sixteen), Tanzania
(four) and Zambia (five). In
addition, the Royal Thai Police
Force ordered three, and the
Uganda Police Air Wing one.
Seven development aircraft were
built, two for Canadian government
evaluation and five YAC-1s for the
US Army. The US Army Caribou
were originally designated AC-1
and AC-1A, becoming CV-2A and
CV-2B in 1962; the latter version
had a higher all-up weight. All
existing US Army Caribou were
transferred on 1 January 1967 to
the US Air Force, when they were
again redesignated as C-7A and
C-7B respectively. Production of
the Caribou ended in late 1973.

21 De Havilland Canada DHC-5 Buffalo

Despite its high-mounted tailplane,
new engines and even more 'utility'
appearance, the Buffalo is quite
clearly a product of the same design
thought which produced the Caribou STOL transport. Structurally,
however, the Buffalo does not have
much in common with its stable-
mate, although it, too, was designed
as a tactical support transport for
combat areas. Its fuselage is much
larger, enabling it to lift not only
greater loads but a greater variety of
loads than the Caribou. The US
Army was envisaged as the largest
potential customer, to whose May
1962 requirement the project origin-

ated as the Caribou II. The cabin has accommodation for 41 troops or 35 paratroops, or for 24 stretchers and 6 sitting patients. Palletised loads weighing up to 7,500 lb (3,400 kg) can be air-dropped. The prototype Buffalo flew on 9 April 1964, and a year later the US Army began evaluation of this and three other prototypes which were designated YAC-2 (later YCV-7A and eventually C-8A). Two of these were assigned to operations in Vietnam in late 1965. Fifteen were completed as CC-115s, with 3,055 ehp CT64-820-1 engines and a nose radome increasing overall length by 1 ft 8 in (0·51 m), for No. 424 Squadron of the CAF's Air Transport Command, to whom deliveries were made during 1967–68. During 1969–70 a total of twenty-four Buffaloes were delivered to the Fórça Aérea Brasileira, and in 1971–72 delivery took place of sixteen ordered by the Fuerza Aérea del Peru. In 1974 a further fifteen Buffalos were ordered by Ecuador (two), Zaïre (six), and Zambia (seven).

22 Fairchild C-123 Provider
The number of transport aeroplanes that have successfully been evolved from gliders is extremely small, yet one such aircraft still playing an important transport role is the Fairchild Provider. The designation XC-123 was applied to an aeroplane, then known as the Avitruc, developed by Chase Aircraft from its experimental wartime glider, the XCG-20, and flown for the first time under power on 14 October

1949. After five pre-production C-123Bs had been completed in 1963, further development of the C-123 was undertaken by Fairchild which built three hundred and two C-123B Providers for the US Air Force. The first production example was flown on 1 September 1954 and the Provider entered US Air Force service in July 1955. Providers were also supplied to the air forces of Saudi Arabia (six), Thailand (four) and Venezuela (eighteen). The Provider's internal capacity is sufficient for 60 armed troops or a 24,000 lb (10,886 kg) freight load, and its squat landing gear and upswept rear fuselage are ideal for tail-ramp loading. In Vietnam, in particular, where more than fifty were used by TAC's 315th Air Commando Group near Saigon, the Provider's STOL and rough-strip performances made it a leading tactical airlift vehicle in the muddy, obstacle-strewn jungle airstrips which were its usual haunt. Another task which befell the Provider was the defoliation of jungle areas suspected of being Viet Cong hide-outs. A large tank amidships dispensed the defoliation liquid via spray nozzles under the wings and tail of the aircraft; operations were frequently carried out at night, with flares dropped from the Provider first to illuminate the target area. This hazardous but effective task was only one of many duties, ranging from artillery movements to the dropping of food and other essential supplies, which were carried out by the Provider. After the cease-fire in Vietnam in 1973, ighty-two Providers were presented o Royal Khmer Aviation, the air orce of Cambodia. Fairchild also puilt one YC-123H, a version with vider-track landing gear. This was itted in 1962 with two underwing auxiliary CJ610 jet engines, flying n this form for the first time on 30 uly 1962. It was followed during 966–69 by the modification of one aundred and eighty-three Providers o a similar configuration, but with ,850 lb (1,293 kg) st J85-GE-17 auxiliary turbojets instead of the less bowerful CJ610s. These aircraft, ised principally in Vietnam, were lesignated C-123K. Ten other 'roviders were re-designated C-123J vhen fitted with Fairchild J44-R-3 vingtip jet engines. The US Coast 3uard uses a C-123B variant, the C-123B, equipped with APS-42 earch radar in an extended nose one.

3   Aeritalia G222

Like most current products of the talian aviation industry, the G222 – vhich is the largest indigenous lesign currently being manufactured n that country – has taken a long ime to come to fruition. It origina-ed from a research contract awarded o the former Fiat company in the pring of 1963, and the design was nitially proposed in four different nission configurations. Three of hese progressed no further than the tatus of research projects, but levelopment was authorised of the ourth proposal, the G222 TCM eneral-purpose military transport. The two flight test prototypes made heir first flights on 18 July 1970 and

22 July 1971 respectively; a struc-tural test airframe was also com-pleted. Service evaluation by the Italian Air Force began in December 1971, and in 1974 the Italian govern-ment confirmed an order for the first twelve of forty-four production G222s to equip two transport wings of the AMI. Deliveries were due to begin in the summer of 1975. Two others have been ordered by the Argentine Air Force. Production is a collaborative effort, with Aermacchi building the outer wing panels, Piaggio the wing centre-section and SIAI-Marchetti the tail assembly. The G222 is conventional in design, having a high-mounted wing and an upswept rear fuselage incorporating a rear-loading ramp/door in the underside which can be opened in flight for troop or cargo dropping. The circular-section fuselage, of approx 8 ft (2·44 m) internal diameter, has a main cabin 28 ft $1\frac{3}{4}$ in (8·58 m) long, with a volume of 2,613 cu ft (74·0 cu m). In addition to a crew of 3 or 4, this can ac-commodate up to 44 troops, 32 paratroops, 36 stretchers and 8 sitting casualties or medical at-tendants, various artillery pieces or military vehicles, or a maximum freight payload of 19,840 lb (9,000 kg).

24   Hawker Siddeley 748 and
    Andover
Since the first flight, on 24 June 1960, of this medium-range passen-ger transport, it has made encourag-ing headway in sales to commercial operators in many parts of the world (see the *Airliners since 1946*

volume in this series). It has also been adopted by military air arms as a personnel transport or crew trainer. Based on the civil 748 Series 2, the version in service with RAF Air Support Command is known as the Andover CC. Mk 2; two form part of The Queen's Flight, and four others have VIP interiors for use as general staff transports. The Royal Flight of the Royal Thai Air Force has two HS 748s, twelve have been ordered by the Fórça Aérea Brasileira, three by the Belgian Air Force, four by the Colombian Air Force, three by the Ecuadorean Air Force, one by the Nepal Royal Flight and two by the Zambian Air Force Presidential Flight. Others were ordered by the governments of Argentina (one), Brunei (one), Germany (seven), Tanzania (one) and Venezuela (one). After assembling four 748 Series 1s from components supplied from Great Britain, the Kanpur Division of Hindustan Aeronautics continued with forty-one Series 2s for the Indian Air Force. HAL also flew, on 16 February 1972, the prototype of a military freighter version. The Indian-built aircraft have 2,105 ehp Dart Mk 531 engines. The Royal Australian Air Force placed an order for ten aircraft in December 1965. Two of these are used as C. Mk2 VIP or standard personnel transports, while the other eight are fitted out as T. Mk 2 flying class-rooms for training RAAF navigators. Two others were ordered by the Royal Australian Navy.

When the RAF began looking in the latter 1950s, for a new short to medium-range tactical transport the British government stipulated that this need should be met by adapting the Hawker Siddeley 748 More powerful engines were necessary, because of the heavy military loads involved; their larger-diameter propellers entailed moving the engine nacelles some 18 in (46 cm) further out on the wing but more important, reduced still further the ground clearance available on what was, and had to remain, a low-wing aeroplane. This problem was solved with room to spare, for another feature of the Andover C. Mk 1, as this version of the 748 is known, is its unique landing gear. This is adjustable over a 3 ft (0·91 m) range so that the Andover can raise or lower its fuselage floor to the level of the cargo being loaded or unloaded; by this means it can 'kneel' to bring the fuselage floor as little as 3 ft 9 in (1·14 m) from ground level. The Andover C.1 is longer than the standard 748, has a strengthened floor, an integral cargo door/loading ramp in the upswept rear end, more internal fuel and redesigned vertical tail surfaces. Internal capacity ranges from 44 troops to 30 paratroops, 18 stretchers (plus attendants), or a 13,500 lb (6,125 kg) freight load. The prototype, converted from a standard HS 748, flew for the first time on 21 December 1963, and was followed by the first of thirty-one production aircraft (XS594) on 9 July 1965. These began to be delivered later in the same year, subsequently equipping No. 46 Squadron of RAF Air Support Command in the UK and No. 84 Squadron in the Persian Gulf.

25 Transall C-160

The C-160 was an international collaboration between France and Germany, who began to compare notes on a joint requirement in the late 1950s, when both needed a tactical and strategic transport aircraft to replace the Nord Noratlas. The name Transall was derived from *Trans*porter *All*ianz, and design and production was shared between the two countries, with VFW-Fokker of Germany as overall production manager. The Tyne engines were built jointly by a four-nation consortium. The first of three flying prototypes was flown on 25 February 1963, and the first of six pre-production C-160As (three for each air force) on 21 May 1965. Production orders comprised one hundred and ten C-160Ds for the Luftwaffe (first flight 2 November 1967), fifty C-160Fs for the Armée de l'Air (first flight 13 April 1967), and nine C-160Zs (first flight 28 February 1969) for the South African Air Force. German and French units to equip with Transalls were, respectively, Lufttransportgeschwadern 61 and 63, and the 61e Escadre de Transport; production was completed in October 1972. The SAAF aircraft are operated by Nos. 25, 28 and 44 Squadrons. In June 1971 the first two of twenty C-160Ds were supplied by Germany to the Turkish Air Force. Four C-160Fs were modified to C-160P in 1972–73 for civilian mail transport in France. The C-160 has a first-class short-field STOL performance, and an excellent carrying capacity. Typical tactical payload is 8 tonnes (which can be doubled over short ranges); alternatively, up to 93 troops, 81 paratroops or 62 stretchers can be transported. The effective cargo volume of the Transall's fuselage is 4,940 cu ft (139·9 cu m).

26 Grumman C-2 Greyhound

To meet a US Navy requirement for a COD (Carrier On-board Delivery) supply transport, Grumman modified its basic E-2 Hawkeye design (which see) in similar fashion to its earlier adaptation of the S-2 Tracker into the C-1 Trader. The process consisted basically of mating the wings, powerplant and tail unit (without dihedral) of the E-2A with a new and enlarged fuselage, provided with a ramp and loading doors at the rear and capable of accommodating a variety of palletised or other cargo, up to a maximum of 10,000 lb (4,535 kg), 20 stretchers and 4 attendants, or up to 39 passengers. The first of two flying prototypes was flown on 18 November 1964, and delivery of an initial batch of seventeen C-2A Greyhounds was made during 1966–68, the first operator (December 1966) being Squadron VRC-50. Delivery of a further seven C-2As was completed in 1971. The Greyhound carries a flight crew of 2, has similar all-weather capability to the Hawkeye, and can be catapulted from, and make arrested landings on, current types of US aircraft carrier.

27 Nord Noratlas

Employing the cargo pod and twin tailboom layout first proved on the Fairchild C-82 and C-119 and seen more recently in the Hawker Siddeley Argosy, the Noratlas was probably used more extensively in Europe than any other short/medium range tactical transport since the mid-1950s. It originated from the SNCA du Nord 2500 prototype (F-WFKL), first flown on 10 September 1949, although the true prototype, the Nord 2501 (F-WFRG), did not fly until 28 November 1950. This differed chiefly in having Bristol Hercules radial engines instead of its predecessor's SNECMA-built Gnome-Rhônes. Three N2501 pre-series aircraft were ordered for evaluation by the Armée de l'Air, the first of these making its first flight on 10 September 1952. Delivery of an initial batch of forty N2501s to the Armée de l'Air was completed on 25 June 1954, and follow-on orders eventually raised to two hundred the total number of this version for the French Air Force. They served widely with units of COTAM (Commandement du Transport Aérien Militaire), and many were still in service at the beginning of the 1970s. The other major operator of the N2501 was the Federal German Luftwaffe, with which it entered service in 1958. Twenty-five were assembled in Germany from French-built components, and a further one hundred and thirty-six were built in Germany by the Nordflug consortium; these bore the designation N2501D, the first flight by a German-built Noratlas taking place on 6 August 1958. Thirty N2501s were supplied to the Israeli Air Force and twelve to the Portuguese Air Force; ex-German and French Noratlases were sold to the Central African Republic (about ten), Chad, Niger (four) and Nigerian air forces. The central fuselage pod, the doors of which are removable for air-dropping of loads, can accommodate 45 soldiers, 36 paratroops, 18 stretchers, various artillery pieces and/or army vehicles, or equivalent freight.

Variants included the N2502 civil passenger transport, operated by UAT (seven) and Air Algérie (three); six of the UAT aircraft later went to the Portuguese Air Force. One N2503, converted from the prototype N2501, was flown with Pratt & Whitney R-2800-CB17 engines; the N2504 (five built, first flight 17 November 1958) was an anti-submarine warfare training version for France's Aéronavale; the N2506, first flown 20 August 1957, was a proposed assault version with slotted flaps, air brakes, telescopic main landing gear and low-pressure tyres, production plans for which were cancelled in a subsequent budget cutback. The N2508, of which two were completed (one serving briefly with Kalinga Air Lines), had 2,500 hp R-2800-CB17 engines. These two aircraft were allocated later as systems testbeds for the Transall

C-160 transport. All of these variants had a Turboméca Marboré auxiliary jet engine at each wingtip. The projected N2505, N2507, N2509 and N2510 versions were never built.

28 Rockwell International OV-10 Bronco

Although employed predominantly by the US Air Force, the Bronco was the outcome of a LARA (Light Armed Reconnaissance Aircraft) design competition announced by the US Navy at the end of 1963. From a number of competing designs the North American NA-300 was selected in the following August, and a development contract followed for seven YOV-10A evaluation aircraft. The first of these was flown on 16 July 1965, each of the first four aircraft having a 30 ft 0 in (9·14 m) wing span and 600 shp T76-GE-6/8 engines. The seventh YOV-10A was fitted with Pratt & Whitney T74 turboprops, but it was the sixth aircraft which eventually set the standard for the initial production version by having uprated T76 engines, a 10 ft 0 in (3·05 m) increase in wing span, anhedral on the stub wings which provide four of the aircraft's seven external stores stations, and several other detail changes. There were changes also to the original specification, involving the installation of a self-sealing fuel system and armour protection for the 2-man crew, with the result that flight testing of the production configuration did not begin until March 1967, some 5 months after the placing of the initial production con-

tracts. The first production OV-10A was flown on 6 August 1967. By April 1969 one hundred and fifty-seven OV-10As had been built for the USAF, ninety-six for the US Marine Corps and eighteen for the US Navy. Production then ended, but was resumed later in the year to fulfil orders for six OV-10Bs and twelve OV-10B(Z)s for the Federal German government and thirty-two OV-10Cs for the Royal Thai Air Force. The first OV-10B was flown on 3 April 1970. The OV-10B(Z), which flew for the first time on 3 September 1970, was purchased for target-towing duties. It differs in having a dorsally-mounted pod containing a 2,950 lb (1,338 kg) st General Electric J85-GE-4 turbojet engine to boost performance. Plans for the remaining eleven to be fitted in Germany with this installation had not been implemented up to 1974. The first OV-10C was flown on 9 December 1970. Deliveries of the OV-10A to the USAF and USMC began in February 1968, the first units to become operational with Broncos being the 19th Tactical Air Support Squadron (August 1968) and VMO-2 (July 1968) respectively, both in Vietnam. In combat, the Bronco has proved itself an able and versatile performer, pleasant to fly, easy to manoeuvre and capable of withstanding considerable battle damage. As already indicated, the OV-10A has two stub-wings sprouting from the lower fuselage; these have four built-in 0·30 in machine-guns, and four attachment points for a total of up to 2,400 lb (1,088 kg) of externally-mounted weapons. A fifth stores point on the fuselage centre-line can carry a 1,200 lb (544 kg) load, and provision exists for a 500 lb (227 kg) capacity station under each wing so long as a maximum weapons load of 3,600 lb (1,632 kg) is not exceeded. The stub-wings and armament capability are omitted from the OV-10B, though an auxiliary fuel tank can be carried on the centre-line station; the OV-10C is basically similar to the OV-10A but does not have the provision for underwing stores. Two night-flying 'gunship' aircraft, designated YOV-10D, were built in 1970 for evaluation by the USMC, and twenty-four OV-10As are to be brought up to OV-10D standard. A number of other OV-10As were allocated for conversion under the USAF's Pave Nail programme for night forward air control and strike duties. The most recent orders have included sixteen OV-10Es (similar to the A) for the Venezuelan Air Force, and sixteen for the Indonesian Air Force.

29 **Grumman OV-1 Mohawk**
When the first mock-up of the Mohawk (then known as the AO-1) was completed in 1957, the aircraft had a single fin and rudder with a high-mounted tailplane; the change to the present twin unit was one of several improvements made before the first Mohawk (57–6463, one of nine YAO-1AF test aircraft, later redesignated YOV-1A) was flown on 14 April 1959. The Mohawk's main function is to provide observation and reconnaissance cover for the US Army, although it is fully capable of more active participation in land engagements. It can operate in all weathers, and from grass fields and short, unprepared emergency landing strips, thanks to an excellent STOL performance; it has been described as 'very hard to upset aerodynamically'; and the large forward-mounted cabin for the 2-man crew affords a generous field of vision in all directions. There were four basic models. The OV-1A (sixty-four built) has a 42 ft 0 in (12·80 m) wing span and is equipped with standard-type aerial reconnaissance cameras; the OV-1B (one hundred and one built) has a 6 ft 0 in (1·83 m) greater wing span and carries sideways-looking airborne radar, for terrain mapping, in a long, torpedo-like pod slung beneath the lower starboard side of the fuselage; the OV-1C (one hundred and thirty-three built) is similar to the OV-1A but with infrared surveillance equipment; and the OV-1D (thirty-seven built), with the extended wings of the OV-1B, is a version capable of rapid interchange from infra-red to SLAR capability, so fulfilling the roles of both the B and C models. The Mohawk entered service in 1962, and production ended in December 1970. For offensive missions, the Mohawk has four underwing attachment points on which napalm or fragmentation bombs, anti-tank weapons or auxiliary fuel tanks, up to a maximum load of 3,740 lb (1,696 kg), can be carried. The US Army has plans to update a substantial number of B and C model

Mohawks to OV-1D standard, and about 16 other OV-1Bs to EV-1E electronic intelligence aircraft. Mohawks are also involved in a number of other Army programmes intended to extend its ECM capability.

30 Grumman S-2 Tracker, C-1 Trader and E-1 Tracer

The Tracker, in service with the US Navy since February 1954, combined for the first time in one aeroplane the dual roles of submarine hunter and killer, formerly undertaken by two separate aircraft. Following the flight of the first of two XS2F-1 prototypes (originally called the Sentinel) on 4 December 1952, Grumman completed one thousand one hundred and eighty-four production Trackers, many for export, and the type has also formed the basis for the C-1 Trader transport and the E-1 Tracer early warning aircraft. De Havilland Canada built a hundred Trackers (forty-three CS2F-1 and fifty-seven CS2F-2/-3), some of these also being exported. The Grumman S-2A, of which seven hundred and fifty-five were built, was delivered to the US Navy and was also supplied to the Aviación Naval of Argentina (six), the Japan Maritime Self Defence Force (sixty), the Netherlands' Koninklijke Marine (twenty-four, plus seventeen CS2F-1), the Fôrça Aérea Brasileira (thirteen CS2F-1), and the Aeronautica Militare Italiano (forty-eight). Other Trackers have been supplied to Taiwan (nine), Thailand, Turkey (fourteen) and Uruguay (three). S-2B was the US Navy designation

of the S-2A when modified to carry Jezebel and Julie acoustic search and echo ranging equipment; some were further updated, in later years, and redesignated S-2F. Seventy-seven S-2Cs were built, with an extruded, offset weapons bay: most of these were later converted to US-2C and RS-2C for utility and reconnaissance roles respectively. The major US versions in more recent use are the S-2D, which appeared in 1959, and the S-2E. The S-2D featured a 1 ft 6 in (0·46 m) fuselage extension, enlarged tail surfaces and a 2 ft 11 in (0·89 m) increase in wing span. Production of one hundred S-2Ds for the USN was undertaken, the first example making its maiden flight on 21 May 1959. The S-2D's equipment includes ECM gear in wingtip housings, sonobuoys stowed in the rear of the engine nacelles, six underwing stores stations in addition to the internal weapons bay, and a retractable MAD 'sting' in the tail. It has an endurance of about 9 hours and carries a 4-man crew. Production of the Tracker continued until 1968 with the S-2E, a development of the D having the Jezebel/Julie combination of location and attack systems. Two hundred and fifty-two S-2Es were built, including fourteen ordered by the Royal Australian Navy as Gannet replacements. Altogether the US Navy operated at least eighteen S-2D/S-2E squadrons; many S-2Es were later converted to S-2Gs, with updated equipment. The Canadian Trackers (now redesignated CP-121) equipped squadrons VU 32, VU 33 and VS 880 of the Royal Canadian Navy, and the fourteen S-2Es of the Royal Australian Navy were delivered to No. 816 Squadron.

In 1957 there entered service with the USN a transport derivative of the S-2D, the C-1A (originally TF-1) Trader. First flown in January 1955, this was an interim COD (Carrier On-board Delivery) transport pending delivery of the C-2A Greyhound (which see), and had a deeper, wider fuselage accommodating nine passengers or a 3,500 lb (1,587 kg) freight load. Eighty-seven production aircraft were built, equipping three Flight Logistics Support and Transport Squadrons of the US Navy. Four of these aircraft were modified to EC-1A for ECM duties.

Following the first flight on 1 March 1957 of an aerodynamic prototype, Grumman also built eighty-eight production examples of the E-1B (originally WF-2) Tracer, an airborne early warning aircraft for the USN, based upon the airframe of the C-1A. This was distinguishable by its triple-fin-and-twin-rudder tail assembly and the huge oval dorsal fairing for its APS-82 search radar. Deliveries of E-1Bs were made from 1958 to US Navy Squadrons VAW-11 and VAW-12, for deployment with various Carrier Air Wings pending the entry into service of the E-2A Hawkeye (which see) in the mid-1960s.

31   Breguet Atlantic

The Atlantic, successor to the Neptune in the maritime patrol class for NATO air forces, represented the first true multi-nation aeroplane to gain service acceptance. Fourteen nations took part in its original planning, and the design was selected over two dozen others submitted. Three years later to the day, on 21 October 1961, the first prototype made its maiden flight. Entry of the Atlantic into squadron service was protracted, partly due to an inadequate number of prototypes being procured. Originally, only two were ordered; a third, 3 ft 3¼ in (1·00 m) longer, was completed to pre-production standard when prototype No. 2 crashed during a test flight. This first flew on 25 February 1963, and was later joined by a second pre-production aircraft. These were followed by orders for forty for France's Aéronavale (Flottilles 21F, 22F and 24F) and twenty for the German Bundesmarine (Marinefliegergruppe 3), the first for each service being delivered in December 1965. In mid-1968, nine Atlantics were ordered by the Royal Netherlands Navy, and the Italian Navy subsequently ordered eighteen. The last four of the initial sixty, and five from the second production run, completed the Dutch order. Then followed those for Italy, delivered to the 41° Stormo Antisom, and finally four others to complete the original French order. Dutch designation of the Atlantic, which serves with No. 321 Squadron of the Marineluchtvaartdienst, is SP-13A. The Atlantic's low-mid wing position, combined with a 'double-bubble' fuselage, leaves the upper half of the fuselage, which is pressurised, uncluttered by structural interference, and here the aircraft's 'operations room' is situated. The 29½ ft (9·00 m) weapons bay in the unpressurised lower fuselage can hold an impressive assortment of standard NATO stores – mines, depth charges, homing torpedoes, bombs, flares and sonobuoys – while there are underwing points for four air-to-surface missiles. The French CSF search radar is in the retractable 'dustbin' aft of the nosewheel bay; there is an MAD (magnetic anomaly detector) in the tail boom, and an ECM (electronic countermeasures) pod on top of the fin. A crew of 12 is carried normally, with provision for a full relief crew to be carried for extra-long missions. The Atlantic has a maximum endurance of 18 hours at 195 mph (320 km/hr) patrol speed.

Manufacture of the eighty-seven production Atlantics ended in July 1974. Later that year the Aéronavale agreed to sell three of its Atlantics to Pakistan, and also authorised development of an Atlantic Mk 2. The second pre-production aircraft will be converted as the Mk 2 prototype, by installing updated and more comprehensive equipment for attacking both submarines and surface shipping targets. It is expected to fly in 1976.

32 Grumman E-2 Hawkeye

The name of Fennimore Cooper's famous American hero is an apt choice for the Grumman E-2, even though the airborne Hawkeye does not carry a single gun. The E-2 is the lynch-pin of the US Navy's Airborne Tactical Data System, the initial E-2A production model having been delivered in 1964–67 for service with VAW-11 in the Pacific and VAW-12 in the Atlantic. Hawkeyes operate in teams of two or more aircraft, flying at altitudes in the region of 30,000 ft (9,145 m) to provide long-range early warning of potential threats from hostile surface vessels and fast-flying aircraft. The key to this system is the powerful search radar, carried in the 24 ft (7·32 m) diameter radome on the Hawkeye's back, which rotates once every ten seconds while the aircraft is in flight. In addition, the substantial fuselage contains detection and digital computers, data link systems and other complex electronics which account for nearly a quarter of the aircraft's total weight. The Hawkeye's radome can be lowered nearly 2 ft (0·61 m) to facilitate stowage aboard the parent carrier. Three systems operators are carried, together with 2 pilots, in the pressurised cabin. Originally designated W2F-1, an aerodynamic prototype flew for the first time on 21 October 1960; a fully-equipped prototype followed on 19 April 1961. The US Navy began to receive the initial production version, the E-2A, in January 1964, and sixty-two of this model were eventually completed, the last being delivered in the spring of 1967. In the same year first details were announced of the E-2B, with enlarged outer fins, improved avionics, provision for in-flight refuelling and other modifications. All operational E-2As were brought up to this standard, beginning in 1969, the first flight by an E-2B taking place on 20 February 1969. This version was serving in 1974 with VAW-113, VAW-116, VAW-125 and VAW-126. A few E-2As have been converted to TE-2A crew trainers. The latest version so far announced is the E-2C, a prototype of which flew for the first time on 20 January 1971. Production began in the following summer, and ten E-2Cs had been delivered by spring 1974. Altogether, twenty-eight E-2Cs are on order, for delivery by the end of 1975; the first unit to receive this version was VAW-123, in November 1973. The E-2C differs from the E-2B primarily in having AN/APS-120, an advanced radar capable of detecting airborne targets in a 'land-clutter' environment. A transport derivative of the Hawkeye, the C-2 Greyhound, is described separately.

33   Lockheed P-2 Neptune

A continuous production/service record of nearly 30 years, at the end of which it was still giving excellent service to the US Navy as well as the air arms of seven other countries, is a measure of the place the Neptune has held in the field of patrol aircraft since the end of World War 2. The first steps towards its design were taken before Pearl Harbor, although the prototype XP2V-1 did not fly until 17 May 1945 and the Neptune did not enter USN service until 1947–48. Intended basically for anti-shipping and submarine patrol, the Neptune has also fulfilled such secondary roles as torpedo attack, minelaying and reconnaissance. The early P-2A to D (originally P2V-1 to -4), no longer in service, accounted for two hundred and thirty-three aircraft (including two prototypes); they were replaced by the P-2E, P-2F and P-2H versions. The P-2E (originally P2V-5, first flown on 29 December 1950), during its absorption into service, gradually introduced such features as a redesigned glazed nose, an MAD 'sting' in the tail, and more modern anti-submarine gear such as the Jezebel/Julie system. The P-2F, first flown on 16 October 1952, introduced a further-modified nose, small tip-tanks, a ventral radome and wider load-carrying capabilities. The P-2H (originally P2V-7, first flight 26 April 1954) offered further equipment and detail changes, and had additional power from two pod-mounted jet engines beneath the wings; this last feature was retrospectively applied to all P-2Es in service, and also to some P-2Fs which, with this feature, were redesignated P-2G. The largest Neptune operator outside the United States was France's Aéro-navale, which had six squadrons of P-2E/F/H. Neptunes also served with the RCAF (one squadron of twenty-five P-2H); the Koninklijke Marine (four squadrons of P-2E/H); the Fôrça Aérea Portuguesa (one squadron of twelve ex-Dutch P-2E); the RAAF (one squadron of twelve P-2H); the Japan Maritime Self-Defence Force (five squadrons of P-2H – seventy-six aircraft, of which forty-eight were licence-built in Japan by Kawasaki); Argentina's Aviacón Naval (one squadron of six P-2E); and the Fôrça Aérea Brasileira (one squadron of fourteen P-2E). Two missile-carrying variants of the Neptune were the MP-2F of the US Navy, armed with the Petrel anti-submarine weapon, and the Dutch P-2H, carrying the Nord AS.12. Overall US production amounted to one thousand and ninety-nine aircraft, including four hundred and twenty-four P-2Es, eighty-three P-2Fs and three hundred and fifty-nine P-2Hs. Argentina, Australia, Brazil, Chile, France, Japan, the Netherlands and Portugal continued to operate Neptunes in 1974.

To replace its P-2H/P2V-7 Neptunes in the 1970s, the Japan MSDF began to receive in February 1971 an improved version of the aircraft designated P-2J. This was developed by Kawasaki from the P2V-7, from which it differs structurally in having a 4 ft 2 in (1·27 m) longer fuselage, redesigned main landing gear and additional rudder area. Licence-built General Electric turboprops replace the original piston engines, and the auxiliary underwing turbojets are of Japanese design. Operational equipment is of a comparable standard to that carried by the Lockheed P-3 Orion, and includes APS-80J search radar in the ventral fairing. An aerodynamic prototype of the P-2J was flown on 21 July 1966, and the first production example on 8 August 1969. Fifty-four were to be built

according to plans announced up to the end of 1974.

34 Lockheed P-3 Orion

When it became necessary to find a successor to the long-lived Neptune for the maritime patrol squadrons of the US Navy, Lockheed decided to base its entry in the official design competition on its commercial turboprop airliner, the Electra. This entry won the competition and, as the P-3A Orion, entered squadron service in August 1962. As compared with the Electra, the Orion's forward fuselage, which includes the internal weapons bay, is some 7 ft (2·13 m) shorter; and it has the familiar MAD 'sting' projecting beyond the tail. The wing and tail surfaces are standard Electra components. Inside the Orion's fully-pressurised fuselage are some $2\frac{1}{2}$ tons of electronics equipment, and accommodation for a crew of 10 on patrols of up to 18 hours. The internal ordnance load may be up to 7,252 lb (3,290 kg), comprising three or four homing torpedoes with nuclear or high explosive warheads, nuclear depth charges, sea mines or other maritime stores. In addition the Orion has ten underwing attachment points for external stores. One of these is normally occupied by a searchlight, but the remaining nine may be utilised for additional mines or torpedoes, rocket pods or Zuni rocket launchers. Initial flight testing was conducted with a modified Electra airframe, first flown on 19 August 1958, followed by a YP3V-1 operational prototype on 25 November 1959. The US Navy initially ordered two basic production models, the P-3A and P-3B. Of these, one hundred and fifty-seven were P-3As, those from the 110th aircraft onwards having more sensitive detection equipment and being known as Deltic P-3As. First flight by a production P-3A was made on 15 April 1961, and the first operational Orion units were VP-8 and VP-44. Four examples of a weather reconnaissance version, the WP-3A, were delivered in 1970. Three P-3As were delivered to the Spanish Air Force in 1973. The P-3B (one hundred and forty-four built) is basically similar to the P-3A except for higher-powered (4,910 ehp) Allison T56-A-14 engines, and this version has also been delivered to the air forces of Australia (ten for No. 11 Squadron), New Zealand (five for No. 5 Squadron) and Norway (five for No. 333 Squadron). Electronics reconnaissance versions for the US Navy, distinguished by large radomes above and below the fuselage and by the absence of the MAD tail-boom, are designated EP-3E (ten converted from P-3As and two others from previously-converted EP-3Bs). The third basic version of the Orion was the P-3C, first flown on 18 September 1968. This entered service in the following year and has considerably more advanced computer-based detection and control equipment. More than one hundred P-3Cs had been delivered by early 1974. One of these was delivered as the RP-3D, a specially-equipped aircraft for oceanographic research with Squad-

ron VXN-8. The P-3F, of which the Imperial Iranian Air Force has ordered six, is generally similar to the P-3C except for some equipment changes.

35 **Canadair CP-107 Argus and CC-106 Yukon**

For many years after the end of World War 2, ocean-going patrol missions for the Royal Canadian Air Force were carried out by modified versions of the Lancaster bomber. By the early 1950s, however, the RCAF began looking for a successor able to cope with the more demanding requirements of maritime patrol, one which could combine the 'hunter' and 'killer' aspects of submarine detection. The aeroplane chosen, the Argus, was the result of much close study and co-operation between Canadair and the Bristol company, builders of the Britannia airliner. The Argus employed the same wing, tail, undercarriage and flight control systems as the airliner, with engines of US manufacture and a completely new fuselage of Canadian design. The Wright Turbo-Compound engines were more economical than turboprops for prolonged low-altitude patrol work, and an unpressurised fuselage was considered adequate. Equipment in the Argus includes search radar in the bulge under the 'chin', a searchlight on the starboard wing, and MAD (magnetic anomaly detection) gear in the tail 'sting'. Two 18 ft 6 in (5·64 m) internal weapons bays each hold up to 4,000 lb (1,815 kg) of mines, depth charges, homing torpedoes, bombs or other stores, and a further 3,800 lb (1,725 kg) can be carried on each of two underwing stations. The usual number of crew is 15. The first Argus (20710) was flown on 28 March 1957, and production ended in July 1960 after thirteen Mk 1 (with US APS-20 search radar) and twenty Mk 2 (British ASV-21 radar, in a smaller fairing) had been built. The Argus entered service in 1958, and equipped Nos. 404, 405, 407 and 415 Squadrons of the Canadian Armed Forces. Developed versions of the Boeing 707 and Lockheed Orion are contenders for an Argus replacement in the latter 1970s.

The Yukon is also descended from the Britannia, although it has a considerably longer, pressurised fuselage. It was developed by Canadair as a civil and military transport, accent in the civil field being mainly on the CL-44D4 cargo version, whose entire tail section can be swung to one side to permit direct loading of freight into the fuselage hold. The Yukon was also used chiefly as a freighter, but with conventional side-loading facilities instead of the swing-tail arrangement. Internal capacity, including underfloor holds, was 7,391 cu ft (209·3 cu m), permitting payloads of 60,000 lb (27,215 kg) or more to be carried. The Yukon was the first propeller-turbine aeroplane to go into production in Canada. First flight of a CC-106 (CL-44-6) was made on 15 November 1959, and a total of twelve was built. Two of these served as passenger transports (convertible to VIP use) with Air

Transport Command's No. 412 Squadron, and the remaining ten, with No. 437 Squadron, Canadian Armed Forces, provided long-range logistics transport facilities for Canadian forces in Europe, Africa and the Middle East. The Yukon was retired from CAF service in 1971.

36 Ilyushin Il-38 ('May')

Probably flown in prototype form in the late 1960s, the Il-38 is a counterpart of the US Navy's Lockheed P-3 Orion, and is in service with Soviet Naval Aviation as a long-range maritime patrol, anti-submarine and electronic intelligence (elint) gathering aircraft. It has been encountered increasingly in recent years over the Mediterranean, North Sea, Atlantic and elsewhere, substantiating reports that it is operational with the Black Sea, Baltic, Northern and Pacific Fleets of the Soviet Navy. This lends strength to the belief that it is now the USSR's principal shore-based maritime patrol aircraft, but it has not yet fully replaced either the Tu-16 or the Tu-95 in this role, and it is worth noting that the Tu-95, which continues to be seen regularly shadowing NATO and other warships, has some 50 per cent greater range than the comparatively modest 4,500 miles (7,240 km) of the Il-38. Like the Orion, the Il-38 owes its derivation to a civil airliner (respectively, the Lockheed Electra and Il-18), and retains – probably with some structural reinforcement – substantially the same airframe and powerplant. Passenger cabin windows are deleted from the fuselage, which has only the few windows needed for observation purposes, and a large under-nose search radar and MAD tail-boom are added. An internal weapons bay is provided for depth charges, sonobuoys, homing torpedoes and other ordnance or operational equipment, and the normal crew is thought to number about 12. To offset the centre of gravity shift created by these internal changes, the wings, which also have hardpoints for externally-mounted weapons or equipment pods, are mounted much further forward than on the Il-18. The Il-38 is believed to have entered Soviet Navy service in early 1970, and about sixty were estimated to be in service by late 1974. The illustration shows one of a small number which operated from Matru airfield, near Cairo, in 1971–72. Although bearing Egyptian Air Force markings, they almost certainly were manned by Soviet crews, and had returned to their Soviet bases by the end of 1972.

37 Lockheed C-121 Super Constellation

This veteran aeroplane dates from the Model 049 Constellation airliner, which had no time to establish itself in the commercial market before the USA's entry into World War 2, when fifteen were delivered as C-69 military transports. After the war the Constellation achieved a deserved success with the world's airlines, and ten aircraft of the Model L-749 type were completed as long range personnel carriers for

the US Air Force. One of these was equipped as a VC-121B with VIP interior, and the remainder as PC-121A standard transports. A stretch of the Constellation resulted in the Model L-1049 Super Constellation with a much increased seating capacity in its 18 ft 4 in (5·59 m) longer fuselage, and the service equivalents of this model included four C-121A VIP transports, thirty-three C-121Cs for the USAF and thirty-two R7V-1s for the Navy. Capacity of the C-121C (and the generally similar R7V-1, some of which became C-121G on transfer to MAC) is 106 passengers, or 72 passengers plus 47 casualty litters with their attendants, or a 40,000 lb (18,144 kg) cargo payload. In addition to the transport variants, there have been numerous radar or ECM picket and AEW versions with Air Force or Navy formations, serving under such designations as RC-121C (for AEW duties; ten built, later redesignated EC-121C); RC-121D (seventy built, some later to EC-121H); C-121J (ex-R7V-1); EC-121K (ex-WV-2); EC-121L (ex-WV-2E); EC-121M (ex-WV-2Q); WC-121N (for weather reconnaissance; ex-WV-3); EC-121P (ex-WV-2); EC-121Q (converted EC-121D); EC-121R (converted EC-121K and P); EC-121S (converted C-121C); and EC-121T (converted EC-121D). The picket versions, distinguished by a large ventral 'guppy' radome and a second fairing, resembling a submarine conning tower, above the fuselage, carry crews of up to 31 men. Other variants have included he EC-121D and H (airborne ighter control) and C-121J (airborne communications relay stations). The Indian Air Force (No. 6 Squadron) operates eight Super Constellations for search and rescue, and one as a transport.

38 Hawker Siddeley Argosy
t took the British aircraft industry nearly twenty years to follow its American colleagues by putting into service a general purpose transport aeroplane with a pod-and-tailboom configuration. The Fairchild C-82 paved the way, followed by the larger C-119 and then the French Noratlas; the fourth, and possibly the last, to follow this layout is the Hawker Siddeley Argosy, which was produced in both civil and military forms. The latter, designed to meet an Air Ministry requirement for a Hastings replacement for RAF Transport Command, differed from its commercial counterpart in having 'beaver-tail' vertically-opening doors at the rear of the cargo pod, and a non-opening nose, at the forward extremity of which was a 'thimble' fairing containing a weather radar. It also featured strengthened wings and higher-powered Dart engines than the civil Argosy 650. The first military A.W.660 (XN814) flew on 4 March 1961, just over two years after the first civil prototype. Fifty-six Argosy C. Mk 1s, which began to enter service in March 1962, equipped two Transport Command (now Air Support Command) squadrons (Nos. 114 and 267) at home, and one squadron

each (Nos. 70, 105 and 215) in the Near, Middle and Far East. Their personnel capacity included 69 troops, 54 paratroops or 48 stretchers with 4 attendants. Maximum short-range cargo payload (29,000 lb; 13,154 kg) included individual pieces of up to 8,500 lb (3,855 kg) in weight, and typical Army loads such as a Ferret scout car or Wombat anti-tank gun. A standard medium range tactical transport, until it was withdrawn from transport service during 1971, the Argosy appeared during its later service life in two-tone camouflage with black under-surfaces, similar to that shown in the Hercules and Andover illustrations in this edition. In 1971 some remained in service with No. 115 Squadron for radar and navigation calibration duties, with the new designation E. Mk 1. Fourteen others have been converted as T. Mk 2 advanced navigation and electronics trainers, for service in this role from spring 1975.

39 Shorts Belfast
On 20 January 1966 the airlift potential of the RAF's key strategic transport base at Brize Norton, Oxfordshire, was augmented by the delivery of the first Shorts Belfast C. Mk 1 to No. 53 Squadron. This huge aeroplane, only ten of which were built, complemented the VC10s of No. 10 squadron at the same base. The Belfast's lower deck can seat 150 troops, and up to 100 more can be accommodated by installing a removable upper floor; but normally the VC10 is employed for all trooping activities, leaving the

Belfast to handle freight movements, for which it was principally intended. Its capacious fuselage can hold a Chieftain tank, three Saladin armoured cars or Wessex helicopters, or ten Land-Rovers, as well as many other possible loads. Although intended mainly for strategic transportation, the Belfast can carry out tactical airlifts as well, having a range of 1,000 miles (1,610 km) with its maximum payload of 78,000 lb (35,400 kg), about double the load of the American Hercules. In this configuration the aircraft's all-up weight is just over a hundred tons. Design work leading to the Belfast began in the middle 1950s as a project for a Britannia development, and the proposal put forward by Short Bros, from which the SC. 5/10 Belfast was evolved, was originally named Britannic. The RAF order for the Belfast was placed in 1960, and the maiden flight of the first aircraft (XR362) took place on 5 January 1964. Since their entry into service the RAF Belfasts have been the subject of a modification programme which included the installation of a fully-automatic triplex blind-landing system – the first application of such a system to an operational military transport aircraft anywhere in the world.

40, 41 & 42 **Lockheed C-130 Hercules**
Since it first entered service in December 1956, Lockheed's versatile and ubiquitous C-130 transport has far exceeded the twelve labours of its Grecian namesake. This middle-sized tactical haulier,

which, say its pilots, is 'built like a truck and handles like a Cadillac' has been built in more than forty variants, serves with as many countries, and fulfils a range of duties far beyond those of its original specification. More than thirteen hundred Hercules had been ordered by the end of 1974, with production continuing. Within the same basic airframe, the payload and performance of the Hercules have increased steadily since the first of the two YC-130 prototypes (53-3396) made its maiden flight on 23 August 1954.

Initial production included two hundred and sixteen C-130As (first flight 7 April 1955), fifteen RC-130As for aerial survey and two hundred and thirty C-130Bs with higher-powered engines and extra fuel. Included in these figures were one AC-130A gunship, two GC-130A drone carriers, eleven JC-130As, a number of conversions to RC-130S for aerial survey duties, twelve ski-fitted C-130Ds (converted from As for USAF Polar supply duties), one NC-130B, five WC-130Bs, seven C-130Fs (converted from Bs for the US Navy), forty-six KC-130F assault transports/refuelling tankers for the US Marine Corps, four Navy LC-130F/Rs on skis, for Polar supply, and twelve search and rescue HC-130Gs, also converted from Bs.

The major production version, for the US forces and for export, has been the C-130E, of which the first example was flown on 25 August 1961. This is essentially an extended-range version, with larger underwing fuel tanks; it entered service in April 1962, and five hundred and nine were built. Apart from those for the US forces, Hercules have been ordered by the air arms of Abu Dhabi (two C-130H), Argentina (three C-130E and five C-130H), Australia (twelve C-130A and twelve C-130E), Belgium (twelve C-130H), Brazil (eleven C-130E and five C-130H), Canada (twenty-four C-130E and five C-130H, designated CC-130), Chile (two C-130H), Colombia (three C-130B), Denmark (three C-130H), Greece (four C-130H), Indonesia (ten C-130B), Iran (twenty-eight C-130E and thirty-two C-130H), Israel (twelve C-130E and four C-130H), Italy (fourteen C-130H), Libya (eight C-130H), Malaysia (six C-130H), Morocco (six C-130H), New Zealand (five C-130H), Nigeria (six C-130H), Norway (six C-130H), Pakistan (nine C-130B including four ex-Iran), Peru (four C-130E), Saudi Arabia (twelve C-130E, ten C-130H and four KC-130H), South Africa (seven C-130B), Spain (four C-130H and three KC-130H), Sweden (two C-130E and two C-130H), Turkey (eight C-130E), Venezuela (six C-130H), South Vietnam (thirty-two C-130A) and Zaïre (three C-130H). Commercial Model L-100 Hercules are operated on behalf of their governments by the Gabon (one), Kuwait (two) and Philippine (four) Air Forces. The C-130H has more powerful engines than the C-130E, which it superseded as the basic production model, but is otherwise generally similar. Accommodation is for a crew of 4 and up to 92 troops,

64 paratroops, 74 stretchers and 2 attendants, or a maximum freight payload of 45,000 lb (20,410 kg). Conversions of the C-130E include the close-support AC-130E (eight built), drone carrier DC-130E, electronics reconnaissance EC-130E and weather reconnaissance WC-130E. Later variants include the USAF Aerospace Rescue and Recovery Service's HC-130H (sixty-three, plus five others for the US Coast Guard) with nose-mounted pick-up gear; the C-130K (sixty-six as Hercules C. Mk 1 for RAF Air Support Command); the search and rescue HC-130N (fifteen for the USAF); the EC-130Q and LC-130R for the US Navy; and the KC-130R for the USMC. Twenty USAF HC-130Hs were modified as HC-130P refuelling tankers for helicopters.

43 Douglas C-133 Cargomaster

The Cargomaster, easily the largest American transport in service prior to the arrival of the Lockheed StarLifter, was built in comparatively modest numbers to provide a small but select force of large logistic transport aircraft for the Military Air Transport Service (now called Military Airlift Command). The original production order was placed in 1954, and the first of thirty-five C-133A Cargomasters (54-135) made its maiden flight on 23 April 1956; deliveries to the US Air Force began in October 1957. With a huge cylindrical, pressurised fuselage capable of transporting an Atlas, Thor or Jupiter missile, the C-133A had an integral loading ramp in the rear fuselage underside, and side-loading doors in the forward fuselage for alternative cargo loads. Its 90 ft (27·43 m) long, 13,000 cu ft (368 cu m) hold could accept 96 per cent of all US Army field force vehicles or equipment. Production of the Cargomaster came to an end in April 1961 after the construction of fifteen C-133Bs, an improved version with uprated engines, a five-ton greater capacity, and clamshell rear doors which added 3 ft (0·91 m) to the usable length of the cargo hold. The first C-133B (59-522) was flown on 31 October 1959. Capacity of the C-133B was more than 110,000 lb (49,900 kg) of freight or 200 fully-equipped troops; a 4-man crew was usual, although on especially long hauls a relief crew could also be carried. A series of accidents resulted in the grounding of the Cargomaster force in early 1965, but by May all the C-133Bs and about two-thirds of the C-133As were back in service. Phasing out of those remaining in service began in 1971.

44 Antonov An-12 ('Cub')
Featuring the high-mounted wing, with marked anhedral, that characterises the whole range of Antonov turbine transports, the An-12 is a freighter development of the commercial An-10A described in the *Airliners since 1946* volume. Both aircraft derived from Antonov's earlier An-8, a smaller twin-engined design which did not achieve widespread service. The chief differences between the An-10A and An-12 lie in the latter's rear fuselage and tail

assembly, which have been redesigned completely with modified vertical tail surfaces and a more upswept rear end incorporating an integral door which is lowered to act as a loading ramp when the aircraft is on the ground. The An-12 is also rare among contemporary military transport aircraft in having provision for a defensive armament, this taking the form of a turret in the extreme tail capable of mounting a pair of 23 mm NR-23 guns. It has been the standard medium-range trooper/freighter of Soviet A-VDV units since the early 1960s, and also serves extensively with Aeroflot. Sixteen were supplied to the Indian Air Force, which used them also in a bombing role in the December 1971 conflict with Pakistan. Others have been supplied to the air forces of Algeria, Bangladesh, Egypt, Indonesia, Iraq and Poland. In 1966 one of the Egyptian An-12s was used as a testbed for the indigenous Brandner E-300 turbojet engine, one of which was pod-mounted in place of the port inner turboprop engine. The hold of the aircraft can accommodate up to 100 paratroops, most Soviet Army vehicles or artillery pieces, or a 'Guideline' missile and its supporting equipment. The crew consists of 5 men. A civil version of the An-12, with the tail gun position faired in, is in service in the USSR and some Soviet bloc countries as a freight transport. Combined military and civil production of the An-12 is reported to have exceeded nine hundred. An ECM version is code-named Cub-C.

45 Antonov An-22 ('Cock')

Just as, in 1959, the Soviet Union stole the show at the 23rd Salon de l'Aéronautique by flying in, unannounced, the world's largest airliner (the Tu-114), so in May 1965 it repeated the treatment by presenting what was then the world's largest aeroplane in any category, the enormous An-22. Flown into Le Bourget by Yuri Kourlin, the first of five prototypes (SSSR-46191), which had begun flight testing on 27 February 1965, completed the Moscow–Paris journey in 5 hours 5 minutes. Although displayed then in Aeroflot markings, it later became apparent that the An-22 is primarily a logistics transport in the same category as the Lockheed C-5A Galaxy, to move missile batteries and large vehicles or equipment loads to and from areas lacking major airfield facilities. The main cargo hold is 14 ft 5 in (4·40 m) square and 108 ft 3 in (33·00 m) long, enabling it to lift nearly four times as much as the RAF's Belfast and permitting the carriage of a maximum *payload* that is not far short of the *basic empty weight* of the Tu-114. Although the production of an aeroplane of this size represents a considerable feat of engineering, the wings and fuselage of the An-22 are, fundamentally, scaled-up counterparts of those on Antonov's smaller transports, the An-10 and An-12. The thin, high aspect ratio wings have double-slotted trailing-edge flaps, and the outer panels have Antonov's anhedral 'trademark'. A large rear-loading ramp/door permits the straightforward loading of cargo, large unpalletised items being hoisted on board by four overhead gantries. The bulky fairings amidships, besides housing the six-wheel main undercarriage bogies, contain the auxiliary power unit (starboard) and the crew doors (port and starboard). A navigation radar is located in the nose radome, and a larger second radome is positioned below and just aft of the nose windows. The An-22 probably entered Soviet Air Force service in 1967, when three military examples were included in the July Aviation Day display. Four An-22s were used to carry relief supplies to Peru in 1970, after the earthquake disaster in that country, and An-22s made seven airlifts to Syria during 1973. The type is also in service with Aeroflot.

46 Tupolev Tu-95 ('Bear')

First revealed to Western observers at Tushino in July 1955, the Tu-95 is the world's first, last and only long-range strategic bomber with propeller-turbine engines, and (save for its civil transport counterpart, the Tu-114) the only large turboprop aeroplane to have sweptback wings. It is comparable in size with America's B-52, and its range is prodigious: Tu-95s regularly patrol both the Atlantic and Pacific oceans, and an unrefuelled range of 7,800 miles (12,550 km) has been quoted by official US sources. Many assessments of the total Tu-95 production have been made, the most likely being between two and three hundred. Of these, about a hundred were estimated to remain in service at the end of 1974 with Russia's long-range strike force, the Dalnaya Aviatsiya. Most of them had by then been converted from their original Bear-A configuration, capable of carrying a 24,250 lb (11,000 kg) bomb load, to Bear-B, modifications including the physical changes necessary to carry air-launched weapons such as a 'Kangaroo' stand-off missile under the belly, the provision of an enormous search and guidance radar in the lower nose, facilities for in-flight refuelling, and a dorsal gun which is believed to fire decoy material to confuse opposing radar. (Armament of Bear-A comprised dorsal, vertical and tail installations, each mounting a pair of 23 mm cannon. The tail guns were operated manually, the others by remote control.) The Bear-B version was first displayed publicly in 1961. The Tu-95 is employed also by naval aviation units of the A-VMF, in several versions for maritime reconnaissance, possibly with all or part of the weapons bay given over to additional fuel tankage. About fifty were thought to be operational with the Soviet Navy forces in 1974. Bear-C has large blister fairings on both sides of the rear fuselage; Bear-D, perhaps the most important version, has a 'chin' radome similar in shape to that of the Canadair Argus, twin rear-fuselage blisters, a very large ventral radome, an enlarged tail warning radar fairing, streamlined tailplane-tip fairings and various other antenna fairings; Bear-E is a reconnaissance version which combines the glazed nose of Bear-A with the refuelling probe of later models, the twin rear-fuselage blisters of Bear-C and -D, and a six-camera installation in the bomb bay; Bear-F has some of the features of Bear-D, but has longer fairings aft of the inboard engines, a modified under-nose radome (or none at all), a lengthened front fuselage, the large ventral radome further forward, no rear-fuselage blisters, and other changes. Another variant is the Tu-114D, produced in small numbers as a cargo or airborne command-post aircraft; despite its designation, this is a straightforward conversion utilising a Tu-95 (Bear-A) fuselage, and not the large fuselage and low wing arrangement of the commercial airliner. The large fuselage of the Tu-114 is, however, retained in a variant code-named 'Moss' by NATO. This is an airborne warning and control version, with modified tail surfaces (including a ventral fin), a huge saucer-shaped radome mounted on a pylon above the rear of the fuselage, an in-flight refuelling probe, several blister fairings along the underside of the fuselage, and another on top of the fuselage, aft of the flight deck. About ten or a dozen of these aircraft were estimated to be in service in 1974, possibly produced by the conversion of existing Tu-114 airframes.

47 Lockheed U-2

There was a story that CIA, officially the initials of the US Central Intelligence Agency, stood also for 'Caught In the Act'; and certainly no aeroplane in history earned the latter description with such world-shaking effect as the U-2 in which Gary Powers was shot down over the Soviet Union on 1 May 1960. Whether or not the U-2 design was actually sponsored by the CIA, there is no doubt that prior to this time it was working on cloak-and-dagger reconnaissance missions, for all its 'utility' category designation and its official description as a high altitude research aeroplane. The U-2 has served principally with the National Aeronautics and Space Administration, and with the 4028th and 4080th Strategic Reconnaissance Squadrons (Weather) of Strategic Air Command in the USA. The U-2 was flown for the first time in August 1955, and before its exposure as a spy-plane had flown from bases as far apart as Alaska, Pakistan, Japan, Nationalist China, Germany and the United Kingdom; there was evidence as late as 1965 that Chinese Nationalist pilots were still being trained in the USA to fly the U-2. Production of the U-2 comprised forty-eight U-2As, U-2Bs and U-2Cs and five U-2Ds. The U-2A has a J57 jet engine with auxiliary fuel in pinion tanks, and is a single-seater like the U-2B and C, which have the more powerful 17,000 lb (7,711 kg) st J75 engine. The U-2D is a 2-seat version of the B. Most of the U-2As – about thirty are thought to have been built – were later brought up to U-2B or C standard. The remainder, for their weather reconnaissance role, were redesignated WU-2A. Among the U-2's tasks in more recent years have been the High Altitude Sampling Programme of upper atmosphere research on behalf of the Defense Atomic Support Agency, and the use of two aircraft by NASA in 1971–72 in connection with the launch of ERTS-A, the first Earth Resources Technology Satellite.

48 Lockheed SR-71

The SR-71, with its impressive and unorthodox appearance, began to be conceived in 1959, under the Lockheed designation A-11, not long before the Powers affair exploded the 'research aircraft' myth of the same company's U-2, and may be assumed to have been evolved originally for a similar purpose – with the important difference that it is built to perform its duties at Mach 3·5. The original three A-11s (60-6934/5/6, the first of which flew for the first time on 26 April 1962) were converted during 1964 as YF-12A prototypes, for evaluation under the US Defense Department's IMI (Improved Manned Intercepter) programme; two of these were responsible in 1965 for several world-class performance records, including the first over-2,000 mph absolute speed record, which was still unbeaten by the beginning of 1975. In addition to its high altitude capability, the YF-12A was designed to carry four Hughes Falcon interception missiles in each of the fairings flanking the long forward fuselage. A fourth aircraft (60-6937) was designated YF-12C, and acted as prototype for the SR-71A strategic reconnaissance version, which has a longer and somewhat cleaner fuselage without the ventral fins of the YF-12A. Both versions are 2-seaters, the accommodation being in tandem under individual cockpit hoods. The first of about twenty-one initial production SR-71As (61-7950) flew for the first time on 22 December 1964, and about a dozen more may have been built subsequently. Strategic Air Command, which began to receive the SR-71A in January 1966, has stated that the 'Blackbird' has repeatedly exceeded the YF-12A speed record since entering service, and can cross the USA coast to coast in under an hour. The first and, to date, only SR-71A unit is the 9th (formerly 4200th) Strategic Reconnaissance Wing at Beale AFB, California. One SR-71B pilot trainer, with reinstated ventral fins and a raised rear cockpit, was also delivered at the beginning of 1966. This aircraft was subsequently destroyed in a crash, but was replaced by an SR-71A, suitably converted and redesignated SR-71C.

49, 50 & 51 McDonnell Douglas A-4 Skyhawk

The little delta-winged Skyhawk was well nicknamed 'the bantam bomber' when it first appeared in the summer of 1954, and in 1975 it was well on the way to establishing an almost certain quarter-century of continuous production and/or service. Up to mid-1973 more than two thousand seven hundred Skyhawks had been built and delivered, and current orders had kept the aircraft in continued production up to the start of 1975.

The Skyhawk came into being, as the XA4D-1, basically as a jet successor to the piston-engined Skyraider, another Douglas design, and the prototype was flown for the first time on 22 June 1954. Early models, before the current A-4 series designations were introduced in 1962, were the A4D-1 (one hundred and sixty-six built, including development aircraft), A4D-2 (five hundred and forty-two built) and A4D-2N (six hundred and thirty-eight built); these became redesignated A-4A, A-4B and A-4C respectively. All were powered by variants of the Wright J65 engine, had a fixed armament of two 20 mm cannon in the wing roots, and three attachments for external stores – one under the fuselage and one beneath each wing. The first A-4As entered service in October 1956 with US Navy Squadron VA-72; the A-4C, with a slightly lengthened nose, was the first model to have limited all-weather capability.

The designation A-4D was avoided, to prevent confusion with the original A4D styling, and the next major production model was the A-4E (originally A4D-5). This introduced a number of important changes, chief among which were the use of a Pratt & Whitney J52 as powerplant and two additional underwing stores pylons, thus increasing both range and effective payload. Four hundred and ninety-nine A-4Es were built, the first example being flown on 12 July 1961. Early in 1965 the US Navy ordered two TA-4Es, a 2-seat operational training version with lengthened fuselage and tandem seating. The production version of this was designated TA-4F: initial orders for one hundred and thirty-nine began to be delivered in May 1966, and subsequent contracts increased this figure to about two hundred. The A-4F, first flown on 31 August 1966, was an updated single-seat attack model with many operational and avionics improvements including a 'saddle-back' humped fairing for avionics aft of the cockpit and armour protection and a zero-zero ejection seat for the pilot. One hundred and forty-six A-4Fs were completed. A simplified trainer version, the TA-4J, was first flown in May 1969 and was still in production in late 1974. The A-4M Skyhawk II is also in current production, and more than one hundred are being built for the US Marine Corps. The A-4M has a more powerful J52 engine of 11,200 lb (5,080 kg) st, deepened cockpit canopy, square-topped fin, brake parachute, increased ammunition for the 20 mm cannon, five external stores points, and a number of other refinements. The first of two A-4M prototypes was flown on 10 April 1970, and deliveries began in the following November.

The gaps in the alphabetical sequence of variants are filled by converted and/or exported versions of the Skyhawk. The Argentine Air Force and Navy have, respectively, received fifty and sixteen ex-USN A-4Bs, these being refurbished aircraft redesignated as A-4P and A-4Q respectively. The Royal Australian Navy received sixteen A-4Gs and four TA-4Gs, of which half were newly-built and half ex-USN A-4Fs and TA-4Fs. The A-4H is a version built for Israel (one hundred and eight, plus ten TA-4H); it is based on the A-4E, but has a brake parachute, square-topped fin and 30 mm DEFA cannon. The Israeli Defence Force has also acquired about thirty A-4Es, at least some of which it converted to A-4F configuration. Ten A-4Ks and four TA-4Ks were exported to the Royal New Zealand Air Force, these corresponding broadly to the American F model and being delivered in 1970. The designation A-4L covers some A-4Cs brought up to A-4F standard for the US Naval Air Reserve. The A-4N Skyhawk II, first flown on 8 June 1972, combines the airframe and powerplant of the A-4M with a twin 30 mm DEFA cannon fixed armament and an updated navigation and weapons delivery system. Intended for export, the A-4N has been ordered by Israel (one hundred and sixteen) and Kuwait (thirty-six). The A-4S is a refurbished version of the A-4B, of which Singapore Air Defence Command has ordered forty. Other countries expressing an interest in the purchase of refurbished A-4Bs at the time of closing for press included Chile, the Lebanon, Thailand, Tunisia and Zaïre.

52 Hawker Siddeley Buccaneer

No separate prototype was ordered of this 2-seat, low-level strike aeroplane, the initial contract, placed in July 1955, being for twenty B.103 development aircraft to meet Royal Navy requirement N.A.39. The first of these (XK486) was flown on 30 April 1958. After carrier trials on board HMS *Victorious*, the first Buccaneer S. Mk 1s were delivered to the Royal Navy in 1961, and the first squadron was commissioned in July 1962. Production of the 7,100 lb (3,220 kg) st Gyron Junior-engined S.1 totalled forty, these equipping Nos. 800, 801 and 809 Squadrons and No. 736 Training Squadron of the Fleet Air Arm. The Buccaneer S.2, first flown on 17 May 1963, has Spey turbofan engines, which give more power, lower fuel consumption, greater accelerating and climbing performance, and a marked increase in range. Eighty-four S. Mk 2s were built for the Royal Navy, equipping Nos. 800, 801, 803 and 809 Squadrons. They entered service in October 1965. The Buccaneer's ground-hugging, under-the-radar penetration role at high subsonic speeds is well known, and its ordnance load may include nuclear weapons or four 1,000 lb bombs on its rotatable internal bay, with additional loads on four underwing pylons. The latter can include 500, 540 or 1,000 lb bombs, Martel missiles or pods of 2 in, 3 in or 68 mm rockets. A camera pack replaces the internal weapons when the Buccaneer is used for reconnaissance missions. Sixteen Buccaneer S.50s for Maritime Command of the South African Air Force were delivered during 1965. These are basically similar to the original S.2, and are fully 'navalised'

although they operate from shore bases; they have a Bristol Siddeley BS.605 twin-barrelled rocket motor in the rear fuselage, which gives a thirty-second boost of 8,000 lb (3,628 kg) st to aid take-off.

In 1969 the hand-over began of most Royal Navy Mk 2s to the RAF, the first RAF unit to be equipped being No. 12 Squadron at Honington, which became operational with Buccaneers in July 1970. These aircraft, delivered initially to Nos. 12 and 208 Squadrons, are designated S. Mk 2A, and have various systems and equipment changes to meet RAF requirements. About seventy ex-RN Mk 2s were converted to this initial standard and will eventually be brought up to S. Mk 2B standard, with the capability of carrying Martel anti-radar missiles, a bulged weapons bay door accommodating an additional fuel tank, and other airframe changes. In addition to these conversions, forty-three new-production S. Mk 2Bs were ordered for the RAF, the first of which made its first flight on 8 January 1970. First RAF units completely to re-equip with the S.2B were Nos. 15 and 16 Squadrons, based at Laarbruch in Germany. Three other S.2Bs (XW986–988) were built for special weapons trials by the Royal Aircraft Establishment, and two RAF aircraft are in use as 'hack' trials aircraft for the Panavia MRCA. Royal Navy Buccaneers still in service (with No. 809 Squadron in HMS *Ark Royal*) are now designated S. Mk 2C without Martel-carrying capability, and S. Mk 2D with Martels.

53 Grumman A-6 Intruder

Chosen in late 1957 from ten other designs, the Grumman A-6 has been well named. The first of eight A-6A (originally A2F-1) development aircraft (147864) flew on 19 April 1960; this aircraft featured downward-tilting rear ends to the engine tailpipes which would have given some 30 deg thrust deflection to aid take-off, but subsequent aircraft have had fixed pipes with a 7 deg deflection. Replacing the veteran Skyraider on US Navy attack carriers, the 2-seat Intruder entered service with VA-42 in February 1963, and by mid-1965 was flying combat missions in the Vietnam conflict, its qualities being well suited to operations in this kind of territory. The Intruder looks deceptively slight for the loads it can carry, but actually is slightly larger than the British Buccaneer, produced for a similar role with the Royal Navy and RAF. For carrier stowage, the Intruder's upward-folding wings reduce the span to 25 ft 4 in (7·72 m), and inboard of the fold lines are four stores stations; on these the aircraft may carry as many as thirty 500 lb bombs, four pods each containing four 5 in Zuni rockets, Bullpup air-to-surface missiles or auxiliary fuel tanks; nuclear weapons may also be carried. There is a semi-recessed weapons bay in the fuselage. The initial US Navy version, the A-6A, is fitted with DIANE (Digital Integrated Attack Navigation Equipment). Four hundred and eighty-two A-6As were built, production of this version ending in December 1969. Subsequent versions have included the EA-6A, A-6B, EA-6B, A-6C, KA-6D and A-6E. The Marine Corps' EA-6A (twenty-one built, plus six others converted from A-6As) acts as an attack escort, using electronic countermeasures to protect the strike aircraft, and itself having a limited ability to deliver strike attacks. The A-6B is an A-6A conversion with improved avionics, permitting the carriage of anti-radar missiles; the first of nineteen examples was flown in 1963. The prototype EA-6B Prowler (149481) first flew on 25 May 1968, this version being an updated EA-6A with a 3 ft 4 in (1·02 m) longer nose and a 4-man crew. Forty-seven were ordered. Both EA models can be distinguished by the large radome mounted on top of the fin. The A-6C, another A-6A conversion, has an under-fuselage turret containing FLIR (forward-looking infra-red) sensors to detect 'difficult' targets, especially at night; twelve A-6As were modified to A-6C standard. The KA-6D is also an A-6A variant, fifty-four of which were produced by converting A-6As; it first flew on 23 May 1966 and is in use as a carrier-borne 'buddy' refuelling tanker. The A-6E (fifty-seven ordered), which first flew on 27 February 1970 and entered service in 1972, represents yet a further updating of avionics compared with the A-6A, and has improved weapon delivery. Most recent version, first flown on 22 March 1974, is the A-6E TRAM (target recognition attack multi-sensor), which carries an under-fuselage package containing infrared and laser equipment in addition to standard A-6E avionics.

54 North American Rockwell A-5 Vigilante

Making its maiden flight in XA3J-1 prototype form (145157) on 31 August 1958, the Vigilante is probably the most advanced carrier-based reconnaissance/strike aircraft in service today in any part of the world. Not long after its entry into US Navy service, with Heavy Attack Squadron VAH-7, in June 1961, the emphasis on the Vigilante's primary role was switched from attack, for which it was originally designed, to that of a Mach 2 reconnaissance aeroplane with a secondary strike capacity. To this end the fifty-five A-5As and six A-5Bs (first flight 29 April 1962) which constituted the first production models were converted to RA-5Cs (the latter before delivery), and a further ninety-one aircraft were built as RA-5Cs. Production ended in November 1970. A unique weapon delivery system was introduced at the outset of the Vigilante's design. This consisted of a tunnel running longitudinally from the central weapons bay, between the two engine tail pipes, and through which the Vigilante's nuclear or high explosive stores could be ejected rearwards. The A-5B (later redesignated YA-5C) incorporated enlarged wing flaps and additional fuel tankage in a hump behind the second cockpit. These features, together with aerial reconnaissance cameras and side-looking airborne radar in a long ventral pack, also distinguish the RA-5C. The first RA-5C was flown on 30 June 1962, and this model entered service in June 1964 with RVAH-5 aboard the USS *Ranger*. Six or more RA-5Cs were assigned to each 'Forrestal' class carrier, and in 1965 two of the smaller 'Midway' class began modernisation to enable them to operate Vigilantes. The Vigilante is operable over a wide speed range in all weathers, at high or low level, and carries a crew of 2. Range may be extended by underwing pylon tanks; in the attack role the four pylons may be used for napalm canisters, 1,000 lb or 2,000 lb bombs, or air-to-surface missiles. In 1971 North American Rockwell put forward to the USAF a proposal for a Mach 2+ interceptor version of the Vigilante, designated NR-349 and having a third J79-GE-10 engine installed in the weapons bay, but this was not proceeded with.

55 Dassault Mirage IV-A

Spearhead of President de Gaulle's much-publicised *force de frappe*, the Mirage IV-A gave to France, from the end of 1964, the means to deliver her own nuclear weapons. This medium range, Mach 2 strategic bomber is yet another variation on the remarkable Mirage theme, a new and advanced design in its own right but based on a scaled-up, twin-engined version of the delta-winged French fighter. Dassault began to design the bomber in 1957, and the prototype aircraft made its maiden flight some 2 years later, on 17 June 1959, powered by two 13,228 lb (6,000 kg) Atar 9 engines. The three evaluation aircraft which followed were very slightly larger, had more powerful Atar 9C or 9K engines and embodied various design improvements, and the first of fifty production Mirage IV-As was flown on 7 December 1963. Towards the end of 1964 these aircraft began to enter service with the 92nd Escadre of the Commandement des Forces Aériennes Stratégiques, deliveries continuing to the 91st Escadre during 1965. A follow-on order for twelve more aircraft was also started in 1965, and all sixty-two had been delivered by 1967. The Mirage IV-A has a 2-man crew, and an unrefuelled range (on internal fuel) of about 1,000 miles (1,600 km); it can, however, operate over much greater ranges by working in collaboration with C-135F tanker aircraft. The main weapon which it is equipped to carry is a 70-kiloton free-fall device and is mounted semi-recessed under the fuselage; alternative loads can include four Anglo-French Martel air-to-surface missiles, or sixteen 450 kg conventional high-explosive bombs under the fuselage and wings. Four aircraft are utilised in a strategic reconnaissance role. Forward of the under-fuselage weapon attachment point is a flat circular CSF radar fairing. The Mirage IV-A can take off normally from runways of 2,625 ft (800 m) length, or can operate out of smaller airfields by the use of up to twelve JATO bottles mounted under the rear fuselage. The Mirage IV-A is currently scheduled to remain in service until the mid-1980s.

56 Douglas A-3 Skywarrior and B-66 Destroyer

The Skywarrior has a long history, having resulted from a 1947 US Navy requirement for a carrier-based attack aircraft to combine jet power with the ability to deliver nuclear weapons. After some 2 years of preliminary design work Douglas was awarded a contract in March 1949 to develop and build two prototypes. The first of these (125412), the XA3D-1, was flown for the first time on 28 October 1952, powered by two 7,000 lb (3,175 kg) st Westinghouse XJ40-WE-3 turbojets in underwing pods. Because of the ultimate abandonment of the J40 engine programme, a switch was made to the 9,700 lb (4,400 kg) st Pratt & Whitney J57-P-6, the YA3D-1 production prototype flying with this powerplant on 16 September 1953. Two hundred and eighty production Skywarriors were built subsequently; these (with their pre-1962 designations in parentheses) comprised fifty A-3A (A3D-1), one hundred and sixty-four A-3B (A3D-2), thirty RA-3B (A3D-2P), twenty-four EA-3B (A3D-2Q) and twelve TA-3B (A3D-2T). The A-3As were delivered from March 1956, the first US Navy unit to receive them being VAH-1. Conversions included five to EA-3A (A3D-1Q), with electronic countermeasures (ECM) gear in the tailcone in place of the A-3A's twin 20 mm remote-controlled guns; one to

YRA-3A (A3D-1P) as a photo-reconnaissance prototype; and others to TA-3A (A3D-1T) dual-control trainers. The definitive Navy version was the A-3B, with more powerful J57-P-10 engines, a modified weapons bay to carry a greater variety of stores, and provision for in-flight refuelling; like the A-3A, it carried a crew of 3. Deliveries of the A-3B, to Squadron VAH-2, began in January 1957, and eventually eight heavy attack squadrons, on board the 'Essex' and 'Midway' class carriers, were equipped with the A-3B. Whereas, in the A-3A and A-3B, only the crew compartment was pressurised, the whole fuselage became so in the three subsequent production models. This was brought about by their specialised roles, which called for 'mission kits' and appropriate additional crew members to be installed in the weapons bay. The photo-reconnaissance RA-3B, first flown on 22 July 1958, thus carried 2 operators and twelve vertical or oblique cameras in this position; the EA-3B, first flown on 10 December 1958, carried ECM equipment and 4 operators, making a crew total of 7; the TA-3B, first flown on 29 August 1959, was essentially an operational trainer for the EA-3B and carried a pilot, 1 instructor and 6 trainees. One TA-3B was converted to VA-3B, equipped as an executive transport. By 1971 those Skywarriors still in service were employed primarily in the electronics reconnaissance role in Vietnam or as KA-3B or EKA-3B flight refuelling tankers.

In February 1952 the US Air Force decided to adapt the Sky-warrior to meet its own requirement for the tactical light bomber and reconnaissance roles. Although considerable internal redesign was involved, additional prototypes were not considered necessary. Instead, the USAF ordered five RB-66A Destroyers for service evaluation. The first of these (52-2828) was flown on 28 June 1954, the most noticeable external difference between the Destroyer and its naval counterpart being the increased-length pods of the engines, which in the RB-66A were Allison YJ71-A-9s of 9,700 lb (4,400 kg) st. Contracts for four production versions of the Destroyer eventually totalled two hundred and eighty-nine, comprising one hundred and forty-five RB-66B, seventy-two B-66B, and thirty-six each of the RB-66C and WB-66D. Destroyer production ended in June 1958 after the completion of two hundred and ninety-four aircraft. The first RB-66B was flown on 4 January 1955, deliveries beginning in February 1956 and eventually equipping three squadrons of the 10th Tactical Reconnaissance Wing in Europe. A few of the early RB-66Bs continued to use the Allison J71-A-9, but most were fitted with the more powerful J71-A-13 of 10,200 lb (4,626 kg) st. This day/night photographic reconnaissance model was followed in March 1956 by first deliveries of the B-66B tactical light bomber, and two months later by the electronics-reconnaissance RB-66C, which had first flown on 29 October 1955. The

RB-66C, carrying a four-men-plus-equipment package in the weapons bay, could be distinguished by radar fairings at each wingtip and beneath the fuselage. The WB-66D, first flown on 27 May 1957, with deliveries beginning in the following month, was a weather reconnaissance version carrying an equipment package and two operators in the weapons bay. Two WB-66Ds were converted in 1962–63 as Northrop X-21A laminar flow wing research aircraft. In the early 1970s the primary role of those Destroyers still in service was, like that of their naval counterparts, the task of electronics reconnaissance in South-east Asia, under designations which included EB-66B, C and E.

57 Yakovlev Yak-28 ('Brewer')

At Kubinka in June 1956, after the Aviation Day display, the Soviet authorities exhibited an attack version of the Yak-25 fighter (the Yak-25R or Flashlight-B) and another twin-jet, swept-wing aeroplane of Ilyushin design (the Il-40) which the western powers code-named 'Blowlamp'. In the event, only the former of these was accepted for service, but at Tushino in 1961 the Russians revealed further developments of the Yak-25 which at first were all believed to be fighters and were given the name Firebar. Three of these machines were alike in having transparent nose stations; two of them (originally Firebar-A and -C) were later recognised to have been light bombers and were given the new code name 'Brewer'. This aircraft is now identified as the Yak-28; the Firebar all-weather fighter, or Yak-28P, is a variant of this basic design and is described in the companion to this volume. The Brewer, via the Yak-26 'Mangrove', thus represents a third-generation development of the original Yak-25 design, in which the wing is modified in planform, has greater area, is mounted higher on the fuselage, and supports larger and more powerful afterburning engines. The fin area is greater, the fuselage noticeably longer, and the main landing gear has a longer wheelbase. The Yak-28 is a 2-seater, has an internal weapons bay which can accommodate a load of about 2,200 lb (1,000 kg) and two underwing store-points for bombs, rockets or guided missiles. Defensive armament comprises one or two 30 mm NR-30 cannon, mounted in the fuselage below and just ahead of the wing roots. The Brewer entered service with Frontovaya Aviatsiya units of the V-VS as an Il-28 replacement in about 1962–63, and is known to exist in at least five versions. Brewer-A, -B and -C are tactical attack bombers, with variations of engine nacelle length, armament and weapon loads; a version with cameras in the bomb bay is known as Brewer-D; while Brewer-E is yet another tactical attack version, with underwing rocket pods and a bulged ECM pack protruding from the bomb bay. The earlier models now appear to be increasingly in use for operational training duties. There have been no reports of Brewer being supplied to other air forces outside the USSR, but some serve with the Soviet Naval air arm, possibly in a torpedo attack or ECM role.

It was known in Western circles in the early 1960s that the Soviet Air Force had in service a high altitude single-seat strategic reconnaissance aeroplane designed to carry out broadly similar functions to those of the American Lockheed U-2. This aircraft, given the NATO code name 'Mandrake', was basically a derivative of the Yak-25 'Flashlight' all-weather fighter, utilising the same fuselage and tail assembly as the Yak-25R Flashlight-B or Yak-26 Mangrove, with a 'solid' nose to house its reconnaissance gear, and married to unswept wings of approx 70 ft 6½ in (21·50 m) span to confer the necessary high-altitude capability. The so-called 'RV' aircraft which set two height-with-payload records in the summer of 1959 was almost certainly a variant of Mandrake, and this assumption, based on the use of two 5,512 lb (2,500 kg) st Klimov RD-9 turbojet engines, indicates that the Mandrake probably cruised at about 475 mph (765 km/hr) at around 60,000 ft (18,000 m). Mandrake, a provisional illustration of which appeared in the previous edition of this volume, was probably intended primarily for Asian or East European border missions where it was not likely to encounter sophisticated interception systems. This explanation appears to be borne out by the location of actual sightings. The aircraft is now thought to have been withdrawn from service.

58 Martin B-57

The innovations and elongations introduced by Martin and other US engineers on the willing Canberra airframe during the past 20 years make it difficult to recognise, in some of the final models, any connection at all with William Petter's original design. After building eight B-57As and sixty-seven RB-57As virtually to the Canberra B.2 pattern (except for a change of powerplant), Martin introduced the first US modifications on its main production version, the B-57B, of which two hundred and two were built. This intruder bomber had a new, 2-man, tandem-seat cockpit, pylons for underwing stores, eight 0·50 in guns in the wing leading edges and a Martin-designed rotating bomb door on which the aeroplane's 6,000 lb (2,722 kg) internal load was carried. B-57Bs were supplied to the Chinese Nationalist, Pakistan (twenty-one) and Vietnamese Air Forces, and a number were recalled from the Air National Guard for active bomber duties in the mid-1960s. Thirty-eight B-57Cs were basically the same aeroplane fitted with dual controls; one B-57C was supplied to Pakistan. Martin then built twenty RB-57Ds, in both single- and 2-seat forms, which had 11,000 lb (4,990 kg) st J57-P-37A engines and a 106 ft (32·31 m) wing span as compared with the original's 64 ft (19·51 m). This model was intended for photographic and electronics reconnaissance duties, and two were supplied to the Chinese Nationalist Air Force; the rest served with Air

Defense Command and the Pacific Air Force. The B-57E designation covered sixty-eight examples of a target-towing adaptation of the B-57B. In June 1964 General Dynamics (Convair) delivered to the 58th Weather Reconnaissance Squadron the first of twenty-one RB-57Fs, a further B-57B or RB-57D conversion with an enormous 122 ft 5 in (37·32 m) span wing, revised vertical tail surfaces, turbofan main engines and two optional auxiliary turbojets in underwing pods. These aircraft, since redesignated WB-57F, were for strategic as well as weather reconnaissance, and for air sampling at extreme altitudes. Further-modified versions of the B-57B, used in Southeast Asia, included the EB-57B for electronic counter-measures and sixteen examples of the Westinghouse/Martin B-57G, which has a much-modified nose section with radar and sensor fairings, laser rangefinder, and infra-red and low light level TV detection gear for night interdiction. The B-57G was also a B-57B conversion.

9   Tupolev Tu-16 ('Badger')

With more than two decades of service life behind it, the Tu-16 has been only partially replaced by the Tu-22 Blinder as the standard medium-range reconnaissance bomber of the Soviet air arms, and some eight or nine hundred were estimated to be still active at the end of 1974. Produced originally for the V-VS's Dalnaya Aviatsiya, or Long Range Aviation, the Tu-16 began in the early 1960s a new lease of

operational life as an anti-shipping bomber with the A-VMF, or Soviet Naval Aviation. About two thousand Tu-16s are believed to have been built in the USSR. The Tu-16 (design bureau designation Tu-88) first entered service with the Soviet Air Force in 1954–55, the first production version being known as Badger-A. Carrying a 6- or 7-man crew, the Badger-A has a built-in defensive armament of twin 23 mm cannon in dorsal, ventral and tail positions, with a seventh gun on the starboard side of the nose; a 21 ft (6·40 m) weapons bay accommodates a maximum 19,840 lb (9,000 kg) war load. About twenty Badger-As, supplied to the Egyptian Air Force, were destroyed in the 'six-day war' of 1967, but were subsequently replaced; six others were supplied to Iraq. A number of Soviet Air Force machines have been converted for the reconnaissance role with additional radar and long-range fuel tanks, and all versions of the Tu-16 so far identified have wingtip-to-wingtip in-flight refuelling capability. Badger-B is a naval conversion carrying two 'Kennel' anti-shipping missiles on pylons outboard of the main undercarriage fairings, and is the model which also equipped two squadrons of the Angkatan Udara Republik Indonesia from 1961. A more extensive conversion is the Badger-C, which features a large search radar in a longer, solid nose, and is a carrier for the 'Kipper' stand-off anti-shipping missile, one weapon being attached beneath the centre fuselage. Pairs of Badgers have frequently been observed on long-range naval patrol, fitted with auxiliary fuel tanks and fairings which contain electronic countermeasures equipment. ECM reconnaissance models so far identified include Badger-D and -E, similar to Badger-C but with various under-fuselage fairings, and Badger-F, which carries ECM pods on wing-mounted pylons but otherwise appears similar to Badger-A. The latest known version is Badger-G, a successor to Badger-B carrying two 'Kelt' rocket-powered anti-shipping weapons on larger underwing pylons. The A-VMF has (1974) about two hundred and seventy-five of this version, and others have been supplied to Egypt. Production of about sixty Tu-16s also took place from 1968 in the Chinese People's Republic, which in 1973 supplied about a dozen to the Pakistan Air Force.

60 Tupolev Tu-22 ('Blinder')

Believed to have flown in prototype form in the late 1950s, and to have entered Soviet Air Force service in about 1964–65, the Blinder is a medium-range tactical bomber and reconnaissance aircraft which has been compared, from a functional viewpoint, with America's B-58 Hustler. Aesthetically and aerodynamically the Blinder is more attractive than the Hustler, though its performance is lower and its range of weapons is more restricted. Knowledge of the Blinder was based initially on the appearance of ten of these aircraft at Tushino in 1961. One of these, since identified by NATO as Blinder-B, was carrying a single 'Kitchen' stand-o[f]f missile semi-recessed beneath it[s] belly. The other nine, which ha[d] numerous under-fuselage ports fo[r] cameras or visual bomb-aiming, an[d] a smaller radar in the nose, wer[e] later dubbed Blinder-A. At Domo[de]dedovo in 1967 the flying displa[y] included twenty-two Tu-22s; thes[e] were mostly of the Blinder-B mode[l] and revealed also a nose-mounte[d] flight refuelling probe. Defensiv[e] armament of the Blinder is limite[d] to a single 23 mm radar-directe[d] gun in the extreme tail. Although i[t] has not replaced the Tu-16 (whic[h] continues in wide-scale service) t[o] anything like the extent first anti[ci]cipated by many western judges[,] the Tu-22 nevertheless is in servic[e] both with medium bomber/recon[n]naissance formations of the Sovie[t] Air Force (about two hundred) and as a maritime strike/reconnaissanc[e] aircraft (and possibly for ECM reconnaissance as well), with shore[-]based units of the A-VMF (abou[t] fifty-five). The maritime recon[n]naissance version, Blinder-C, carrie[s] six cameras in the weapons bay an[d] has detail modifications to the nose cone, dielectric panels and othe[r] features. Blinder-D is an operationa[l] training version, distinguished by its 'stepped' crew enclosure em[-]bodying a raised rear cockpit fo[r] the second pilot. The comba[t] versions are thought to carry a crew of 3.

61 Tupolev Tu-? ('Backfire')

Potentially the most significant new warplane to have been developed in the USSR in recent years, the

Backfire supersonic swing-wing strategic bomber was first detected by US reconnaissance satellite in the autumn of 1969, though up to the spring of 1975 no photograph of it had been published and most of the information appearing in print was necessarily speculative. Admiral Thomas H. Moorer, USN, Chairman of the US Joint Chiefs of Staff, has said that Backfire weighs two and a half times as much as the FB-111 and is about four-fifths the size of the B-1; the weight and dimensional estimates on page 77 are based on this statement. The twin afterburning engines are thought to be based on, or similar to, the NK-144 turbofans which power the Tu-144 supersonic transport; maximum speed is of the order of Mach 2·25 to 2·5 for over-the-target dash; and the maximum unrefuelled range (though Backfire is equipped for in-flight refuelling) is thought to be sufficient for intercontinental operation. Although based substantially upon 1972–73 photographs of a US recognition model, the illustration on page 77 departs from this in one or two respects, chiefly to depict a nose configuration more closely akin to that of the Tu-22 Blinder (Backfire's immediate service predecessor) and a brake parachute or tail warning radar fairing beneath the rudder. Since this illustration was prepared, it has become known that the cockpit has side-by-side crew seating, and it should be stressed that *all* detail in this or any other illustration should be regarded as strictly provisional until genuine photographs of the aircraft become available. The wings, which have variable geometry on the outer panels only, appear to have a typical Tupolev planform (as, for example, those of the Tu-28P fighter or Tu-154 airliner), and carry the traditional main landing gear fairings at their trailing edges. In fact, two versions (Backfire-A and -B) have been reported, the latter with much shallower fairings, which do not protrude beyond the trailing edges of the wings, and increased wing span. If the estimates of Backfire's range are accurate, almost all of the fuselage space would probably be needed for engines, fuel and avionics, leaving little or no space for internal weapon stowage. One possible weapon which has been mentioned is the fairly recently developed ASM-6 rocket-powered stand-off missile, with a quoted range of 460 miles (740 km). It would be consistent with earlier Soviet bomber/missile practice for Backfire to carry one of these under the fuselage, and doubtless external hard-points for short-range attack missiles, or free-fall or other weapons, could be provided on fuselage or inner-wing stations. Alternatively, US official sources have suggested that Backfire appears best suited to a peripheral role, and internal weapon stowage might well be possible on short/medium-range operations if some of the fuel tankage was removed. Twelve development aircraft, possibly comprising two flight-test prototypes and ten pre-production aircraft, were known to exist by early 1973, and it was estimated that about thirty-five Backfires were in operational service with the Soviet Air Force by the end of 1974. The Backfire is also expected to be deployed operationally by Soviet Naval Aviation.

62 Lockheed S-3 Viking

Five of America's major aircraft manufacturers submitted proposals in April 1968 to meet the US Navy's requirement for a replacement for the venerable Grumman S-2 Tracker in the carrier-borne ASW role. In the following August the choice was reduced to the competing designs of General Dynamics (Convair) and Lockheed, and the latter company (in partnership with LTV Aerospace) was finally selected by Naval Air Systems Command to develop the new aircraft. The initial contract called for the completion of six development aircraft (later increased to eight), and up to the end of 1974 US Navy firm orders for the S-3A totalled one hundred and forty-six production examples, of the currently-planned procurement of one hundred and eighty-seven. A full-sized mock-up of the S-3A was completed in 1970, and the first of the development aircraft (157992) was rolled out in November 1971 and flew for the first time on 21 January 1972, nearly two months ahead of schedule; deliveries to the USN for BIS (Bureau Investigation and Survey) testing began in October 1973, followed by the first deliveries of squadron aircraft (to VS-41 for training) in February 1974. The

initial S-3A version of the Viking carries a crew of 4, each on a zero-zero ejection seat; its ASW equipment includes an on-board computer and data processer, and the latest and most sensitive MAD gear, acoustic and non-acoustic sensors, ECM gear and radar. A divided weapons bay in the centre fuselage can accommodate four bombs, mines, depth charges or torpedoes and there is a triple ejector rack beneath each wing for carrying mines, cluster bombs, rocket pods, flare launchers or auxiliary fuel tanks. There is a considerable stretch potential in the Viking's design which will allow for an increase of the gross weight up to at least 50,000 lb (22,680 kg) and of the initial electronics by some 50 per cent. Later versions are foreseen to fulfil such roles as flight refuelling tanker, utility transport, ASW command and control or ECM patrol and monitoring.

63 Dassault Mystère 20/ Falcon 20

Work on building a prototype of this rear-engined light executive aeroplane began in January 1962, and the completed aircraft flew for the first time on 4 May 1963, powered by 3,300 lb (1,489 kg) st Pratt & Whitney JT12A-8 engines. On 10 July 1964 it was reflown with General Electric CF700 turbofans and various structural changes, including an 18 in (0·45 m) cabin extension, a 3 ft 3¼ in (1·00 m) increase in wing span, and a strengthened undercarriage. By 1974 the order book stood at well over three undred of these aircraft, in various series, some two-thirds of them bought by the Business Jets Division of Pan American Airways for resale in the civil market. Military and government orders have so far included eight for the Armée de l'Air, three as aircrew trainers for No. 34 Squadron of the RAAF, seven for No. 412 Squadron of the Canadian Armed Forces, three for the Spanish Air Ministry, two for the Belgian Air Force, two for the Norwegian Air Force, two for the Moroccan Ministry of National Defence, three for the Central African Republic, one each for the Algerian, Jordanian and Pakistan governments, and one each for the Sultan of Oman and the air force of the Ivory Coast. The Falcon, in which Mme Jacqueline Auriol set two international closed-circuit speed records in June 1965, carries a crew of 2 and, in its passenger configuration, normally seats up to 10 people (maximum 14). Two of the Armée de l'Air machines are Falcon 5Ts, with pointed nose radomes and equipped as flying classrooms for operational and navigation training of Mirage III combat pilots. Two similar aircraft were sold to Libya.

4 Kawasaki C-1

Ever since it was re-formed after World War 2, the Japan Air Self-Defence Force has relied for its main transport commitment, apart from a few YS-11As, on the ageing Curtiss C-46 whose origins go back to 1939. That situation will be remedied with the entry into service of the twin-turbofan C-1, twenty-four of which had been ordered by the end of 1974. This figure is expected to be increased by later contracts. The basic design work, begun in 1966, was undertaken by the Nihon Aircraft Manufacturing Company (NAMC), and Mitsubishi completed a full-scale mock-up of the aircraft in March 1968. In the following autumn NAMC began construction of two XC-1 prototypes, which made their first flights on 12 November 1970 and 16 January 1971, and a third airframe for static testing. Service evaluation by the Japan Defence Agency started in the spring of 1971, and was completed in March 1973. The prototypes were followed by two pre-production C-1s (first flight 19 September 1973) and a fatigue test airframe, and in early 1974 three of the four flight test aircraft were with the Transport Wing of the JASDF, at Iruma, for crew training, prior to service introduction in early 1975. The production C-1 is the overall responsibility of Kawasaki, but construction is shared with Fuji (outer wings), Mitsubishi (centre and aft fuselage and tail), and Nippi (flaps, ailerons, engine pylons and pods). Kawasaki is building the forward fuselage and wing centre-section, and is responsible for final assembly and pre-delivery flight testing. The C-1 carries a crew of 5, including a cargo supervisor, and is able to carry up to 60 troops, 45 paratroops, 36 stretchers and medical attendants, Army vehicles and equipment, or palletised cargo up to a normal payload of 17,640 lb (8,000 kg).

65 Ilyushin Il-76 ('Candid')

First flown, by Eduard Kuznetsov, on 25 March 1971, the Il-76 four-turbofan transport made its public debut just over two months later when aircraft SSSR-86712 (see colour plate) was exhibited at the Salon de l'Aéronautique et de l'Espace in Paris. A generally similar aircraft (SSSR-86711) was displayed at the following Salon in 1973, and by the middle of that year four development aircraft were reported to have been completed. Soviet official statements up to the end of 1974 had referred only to proposed civil applications of the Il-76, such as the transport of sections of pipeline for natural gas supplies from Siberia, and other heavy-lift operations in remote areas. However, its similarity to the Lockheed C-141 StarLifter in size (it is slightly bigger and heavier) and configuration make it almost impossible to believe that the Il-76 will not find at least equal employment as a military tanker or transport. Designed by G. Novozhilov, successor to the semi-retired Sergei Ilyushin, the Il-76 has multiple wing high-lift surfaces, clamshell thrust reversers on its four turbofan engines, and 4-wheel nose and 8-wheel main landing gear bogies, all of which contribute to a good short-field performance. With fuel for 3,100 miles (5,000 km) and a reduced payload of 71,650 lb (32,500 kg), it can take off and land on unprepared strips. A crew of 3

(plus an optional loadmaster) ar carried, and loading, aided by mechanised cargo-handling system is via a large three-section rear loading ramp/door under the rear of the fuselage. The entire interior i pressurised.

66 BAC VC10

Brize Norton, Oxfordshire, home of No. 10 Squadron, RAF Air Suppor Command, is the headquarters of the fourteen VC10s delivered to th Royal Air Force during 1966–68 This was the only military order to be placed for a jet transport whose passenger appeal in the civil marke was almost as marked as that of it turboprop-engined ancestor, th Viscount, some dozen years pre viously. The first prototype of th VC10 made its maiden flight on 29 June 1962, that of the first aircra for the RAF (XR806) taking plac on 26 November 1965, with de liveries to Transport Command (a it then was) starting on 7 July 1966 Although basically a standar VC10, with rearward-facing seat for 150 passengers, the Model 110 for the RAF also embodies a num ber of features of the Super VC10 including Conway RCo.43 by-pas engines with thrust reversal on th outer pair, a fin fuel tank, extende wing leading edges and in-fligh refuelling capabilities. Intended pri marily for personnel transport ove long ranges, the Belfast being th RAF's standard heavy freight trans port, the VC10 nevertheless has large forward cargo door and re inforced flooring. Air Support Com mand aircraft, named individuall after air holders of the Victoria Cross, are designated VC10 C. Mk 1. One aircraft was employed from 1969 as a flying testbed for the Rolls-Royce RB.211 turbofan engine. A description of the VC10 and Super VC10 commercial models appears in the companion volume *Airliners since 1946*.

67 Hawker Siddeley Comet and Nimrod

With the Belfast and VC10, the Comets in Transport Command service gave the RAF a highly effective long-range strategic transport force, capable of transferring men and equipment to any part of the world in a short space of time. The Comet force included, at its peak, eleven C. Mk 2, three of which were assigned to No. 90 (Signals) Group but available for transport duty if required; two T. Mk 2 crew trainers; and five C. Mk 4. The C.2s, ex-airline machines which entered RAF service with No. 216 Squadron in 1956, had capacity for 48 passengers, or 36 passengers and 11,200 lb (5,080 kg) of cargo; they were retired in 1967. The C.4s, acquired in 1962 and still serving in 1974, have maximum seating for 94 people in addition to the crew of 5, and have strengthened floors for cargo carrying.

Early in 1965 the British government authorised development of the basic Comet design, as the Hawker Siddeley 801, to provide a maritime reconnaissance replacement for the ageing early marks of the Shackleton. As a first stage, two Comet 4C airliners were converted in 1965–66 to have a modified fuselage with internal provision for search and reconnaissance equipment and accommodation for the crews during long patrols. The first of these prototypes (XV147) was flown on 23 May 1967, and was powered by Rolls-Royce Spey turbofan engines, as specified for production aircraft. The second prototype, which followed it on 31 July 1967, was used primarily to test the maritime equipment and retained its original Avon engines. The major production version is the Nimrod MR. Mk 1; the first example (XV226) flew on 28 June 1968, and deliveries to RAF Strike Command began in October 1969, the first operational unit being No. 201 Squadron. These now serve also with Nos. 42, 120, 203 and 206 Squadrons, and with the ANZUK force from a base on Singapore. Thirty-eight MR. Mk 1s were ordered initially; they were followed by three specially-equipped R. Mk 1s, delivered in 1971 to No. 51 Squadron and officially described as radio/radar calibration aircraft, although they may also be fulfilling an electronics reconnaissance role. In January 1972 it was announced that a further batch of eight Nimrod MR. Mk 1s were to be built for the RAF, which will then have six squadrons equipped with this version. From the Comet airframe, the Nimrod retains largely unchanged the wing and horizontal tail surfaces and, in strengthened form, the landing gear. The fuselage contours are new, and are made up essentially of a pressurised upper shell inherited from the Comet and an unpressurised lower shell containing the weapons bay and much of the maritime equipment. A large dorsal fin has been added, the main fin is topped by a streamlined ECM pod, and an MAD tailboom (not on the R. Mk 1) is fitted. The Nimrod carries a crew of 12, and its 48½ ft (14·78 m) weapons bay can accommodate a wide range of ASW weapons including bombs, mines, depth charges and homing torpedoes. Additionally, a pylon under each wing, just outboard of the main landing gear units, can be used to carry an AS.12 or other air-to-surface missile. Provision is made for the carriage of 45 troops in a secondary transport role. From 1977, the RAF's Nimrod MR. Mk 1s will be updated to MR. Mk 2 standard, with improved avionics and maritime patrol equipment.

68 Hawker Siddeley Vulcan

The transonic Vulcan is the world's largest operational delta-winged aeroplane, and entered Bomber Command service in the middle 1950s. It was designed by the former Avro company, the Avro 698 first prototype (VX770) making its maiden flight on 30 August 1952 powered by four Rolls-Royce Avon engines. The second prototype (first flight 4 September 1953) and subsequent aircraft all had Bristol Siddeley Olympus turbojets. Production of the Vulcan B. Mk 1 began in 1953; forty-five were built (XA889–913, XH475–483, XH497–506 and XH532), the first operational unit being No. 83

Squadron in May 1957. Most B Mk 1s were subsequently modified to B. Mk 1A standard, with electronic countermeasures equipment in a bulged tail cone. By the mid-1960s all Mk 1/1A Vulcans had been placed on the reserve. Their place in the front-line strategic V-bomber force was then occupied by the B. Mk 2, which has a 12 ft 0 in (3·66 m) greater wing spread and more powerful Olympus engines. Deliveries of the Vulcan B.2, which began in July 1960, were made to Nos. 9, 12, 27, 35, 44, 50, 83, 101 and 617 Squadrons, the total number built being seventy-nine (XH533–539, XH554–563, XJ780–784, XJ823–825, XL317–321, XL359–361, XL384–392, XL425–427, XL443–446, XM569–576, XM594–612 and XM645–657). Whereas the Mks 1/1A were able to carry free-falling nuclear weapons or 21,000 lb (9,525 kg) of conventional high explosive bombs, the Vulcan B.2 was equipped also to carry the British powered stand-off bomb, Blue Steel. Both marks of Vulcan were, while in service, re-fitted with successively more powerful variants of the Olympus jet engine, and the Mk 2 with capacity for in-flight refuelling. In 1971 RAF Strike Command still retained two Blue Steel-equipped Vulcan squadrons, but by 1974 all remaining Vulcan bomber squadrons (Nos. 44, 50, 101 and 617 in the UK and Nos. 9 and 35 in Cyprus) were fulfilling an overland strike rather than a strategic bombing role. A seventh Vulcan squadron, No. 27, operates in the strategic reconnaissance role with SR. Mk 2 aircraft, converted from B.2s.

69 Handley Page Victor

The Victor, third of Britain's trio of V-bombers, was first flown in prototype form (WB771) on 24 December 1952; a second prototype (WB775) was flown on 11 September 1954. The Victor became operational with No. 10 Squadron of RAF Bomber Command (now Strike Command) in the spring of 1958. Fifty examples of the B. Mk 1 initial production version were built (XA917-941, XH587-594, XH613-621, XH645-651 and XH667). The first of these flew for the first time on 1 February 1956, and deliveries to the RAF began in November 1957. The B. Mk 1 was powered by four 11,050 lb (5,012 kg) st Armstrong Siddeley Sapphire 202/207 turbojets. Twenty-four B. 1s were built as, or converted to, B. Mk 1A, the latter model differing in internal equipment and in having tail warning radar in the tail-cone. A further eleven were converted to K. Mk 1 in-flight refuelling tankers, and eventually twenty of the B. 1As also were converted for similar duties, fourteen of them as K. Mk 1As and six as B(K). Mk 1As. The second production bomber version, the B. Mk 2, was first flown on 20 February 1959 (XH668); deliveries began in November 1961, and the first B. 2 Squadron (No. 139) was formed three months later. The Victor B. Mk 2 had a 10 ft 0 in (3·05 m) greater wing span, larger air intakes, and 17,250 lb (7,824 kg) st Rolls-Royce Conway

RCo. 11 by-pass turbojet engines. Thirty Victor B. Mk 2s were completed (XH668-675, XL158-165, XL188-193, XL230-233, XL511-513 and XM714-718), production ending in late 1962. From 1963, these were converted to B. Mk 2R (for retrofit) standard, with uprated Conway engines and blister fairings above the outer wing trailing edges. These blisters had a dual purpose, for as well as reducing drag they contained 'window' which could be dispersed in the wake of the bomber to confuse the radar of a pursuing interceptor. The B. Mk 2R was equipped to deliver the Blue Steel stand-off missile, which it carried semi-externally; but it could instead carry, internally, various free-fall nuclear weapons or thirty-five 1,000 lb high explosive bombs, operating at either high or low level. Nine B. 2Rs were later converted to SR. Mk 2 strategic reconnaissance aircraft, serving with No. 543 Squadron. The twenty-one other B. 2Rs are currently (1974) undergoing conversion (by Hawker Siddeley, following the demise of Handley Page) as K. Mk 2 tankers, and this conversion will also be applied to the SR. 2s. The updated K. 2s are to replace the Mk 1/1A tankers of Nos. 55, 57 and 214 Squadrons.

70 Boeing B-52 Stratofortress

Boeing's giant B-52 seems almost certain to go down in history as the last of the big 'heavies', such have been the changes in global strategy since it first entered US Air Force service in the summer of 1955. Certainly the use of a 200 ton, eight-engined, inter-continental bomber to drop propaganda leaflets over North Vietnam was the antithesis of cost-effectiveness, as events demonstrated all too clearly – though nothing could be further from the role which the B-52 was designed to perform. The first XB-52 prototype (49-230) was flown on 2 October 1952, and was followed by a single YB-52, three B-52As and fifty examples of the initial production models, the B-52B and RB-52B. Strategic Air Command had in service in 1974 about four hundred and fifty B-52s, approximately one-third of these being the tall-finned B-52C, D, E and F models (respective production totals were thirty-five, one hundred and seventy, one hundred, and eighty-nine); these differ from one another mainly in such matters as engine power, electronics and other equipment and have a maximum internal bomb load of 60,000 lb (27,216 kg). The remainder are B-52Gs or B-52Hs, of which the former has a marked performance increase and a cropped vertical tail, and was the first Stratofortress model to carry the Hound Dog stand-off missile. Two of these weapons are carried underwing, one between the fuselage and the inner pair of engine pods on each side. The B-52G's internal load can include two Quail decoy missiles and 20,000 lb (9,072 kg) of free-fall bombs, and a tail turret with four remotely-controlled 0·50 in machine-guns protects the bomber from the rear. Decoy rockets may also be carried beneath the wings. One hundred and ninety-three B-52Gs were built, the first example being flown on 26 October 1958 and the first deliveries to SAC being made in the following February. The final version, which first flew on 6 March 1961, was the B-52H, one hundred and two of which were built up to June 1962. This model is essentially similar to the G except that it has 16,000 lb (7,257 kg) st Pratt & Whitney TF33-P-1 turbofan engines, which increase the range and general performance still further, and a multi-barrel cannon in the tail turret. The B-52H has flown unrefuelled for a distance of more than 12,500 miles (20,117 km). All B-52s still in service have been modernised and strengthened structurally to enable them to carry out low-level penetration missions. The Stratofortress is scheduled to remain in service, in gradually diminishing numbers as the earlier variants are phased out, until the late 1970s. Ninety-six G and H models are the subject of a modernisation programme to enable them to carry up to twenty SRAMs (Short-Range Attack Missiles), six under each wing and eight internally. In another modification programme, some two hundred B-52G and H models are being fitted with Hughes FLIR (forward-looking infra-red) sensors in twin under-nose fairings. Another updating programme involves the installation of EVS (Electro-optical Viewing System) night vision equipment in the G and H models.

71, 72 & 73 **Boeing Stratotanker (KC-135), Stratolifter (C-135), VC/EC-137 and E-3A**

The military counterpart of the Boeing 707 airliner, which has the Boeing Model number 717, is in use by the US Air Force in a considerable variety of roles, its total production having amounted to eight hundred and six. By far the most prolific version is the KC-135A flight refuelling tanker, which first flew on 31 August 1956; an overall total of seven hundred and thirty-two KC-135As were built before production ended in December 1964. They have been in service since June 1957, and are currently able to refuel other aircraft by the probe-and-drogue method as well as by the familiar 'butterfly boom' beneath the rear fuselage. The KC-135A can be used as a long-range transport, but there were also specialised transport models. These included fifteen new and three converted C-135As (first flight 19 May 1961) and thirty fan-engined C-135Bs (first flight 12 February 1962), the latter's capacity being 126 troops, 44 casualty litters or 87,100 lb (39,508 kg) of freight. Twelve C-135F tankers, generally similar to the A model, were supplied to the Armée de l'Air to act as a tanker fleet for the Mirage IV-A bomber force. The last USAF production model of the Boeing 717 (seventeen built) was the EC-135C (originally KC-135B) airborne command post. Boeing Model number 739 identifies four RC-135A and ten RC-135B built, respectively, for the Air Photographic and Charting Service of MAC and for electronic reconnaissance.

Aircraft converted for special functions have resulted in many new designations, including EC-135A (six, airborne command post/communications relay), JKC-135A and NKC-135A (special test), VC-135B (eleven, VIP transport), WC-135B (ten, weather reconnaissance), RC-135C (ten, electronic reconnaissance), RC-135D (four, ditto), RC-135E (one, ditto), EC-135G (four, airborne command post/communications relay), EC-135H (five, airborne command post), EC-135J (three, ditto), EC-135K (one, ditto), EC-135L (three, airborne command post/communications relay), RC-135M (special mission), EC-135N (eight, radio/telemetry for Apollo space programme), EC-135P (five, airborne command post), KC-135Q (tanker for SR-71), KC-135R (special reconnaissance), RC-135S (ditto), KC-135T (ELINT collection), and RC-135U (special reconnaissance).

In addition to the above, several examples of the commercial Boeing 707 have been supplied to meet military orders. These have included three short-fuselage 707-153s as VC-137A (VC-137B after conversion to turbofans) and one Presidential 707-353 (VC-137C) for the USAF; and other 707-320 series to the Argentine Air Force (one), Federal German Luftwaffe (four), Canadian Armed Forces (five, designated CC-137), Imperial Iranian Air Force (six), Israeli Defence Force (five), Portuguese Air Force (two) and USAF (one).

Two other Boeing 707-320 airframes have undergone conversion to become EC-137D aerodynamic prototypes of Boeing's new AWACS (Airborne Warning and Control System) patrol aircraft for the USAF. The first of them (71-1407) flew for the first time in the new form on 9 February 1972, and their main purpose was to flight test the large prototype radars developed by Hughes and Westinghouse and mounted in the huge circular radome above the rear fuselage of the EC-137D. After selection of Westinghouse for the radar contract, the second development phase involves four genuine E-3A prototypes, each powered by four 21,000 lb (9,525 kg) st Pratt & Whitney TF33-P-7 turbofan engines. The third (production) phase is dependent upon finance and the outcome of trials during the earlier phases; if approved, it is expected to involve thirty-four aircraft, including the bringing up of the prototypes to production standard.

74 Myasishchev Mya-4 ('Bison')

Considering the degree of attention and speculation that usually surrounds the appearance of any new Soviet military aircraft, comparatively little is known of the four-jet Mya-4 (or M-4) designed by V. M. Myasishchev, though its existence first became known to the west two decades ago. Its first public appearance was in the flypast over Moscow on May Day 1954, in which a prototype, designated TsAGI 428, took part; this is believed to have made its first flight in 1953. Production examples began to enter service with units of the Dalnaya Aviatsiya (Long Range Aviation) in 1955. Of comparable purpose to the USAF's B-52 Stratofortress, the Mya-4 carried a crew of 6, and at least one feature which it shared with the B-52 was a similar undercarriage configuration, with 'bicycle'-type tandem main-wheel bogies in the fuselage, fore and aft of the weapons bay, and outboard supporting wheels housed in the pod fairings at the wingtips. Wing span and length were, respectively, 165 ft $7\frac{1}{2}$ in (50·48 m) and 154 ft $10\frac{1}{4}$ in (47·20 m). Power plant was four 19,180 lb (8,700 kg) st Mikulin AM-3D or AM-3M turbojet engines. The Bison could carry a maximum bomb load in the region of 9,920 lb (4,500 kg), and because of its comparatively low operational ceiling of 45,000 ft (13,700 m) it was equipped for defence with radar-directed barbettes above and below the fuselage, fore and aft of the wings, each with twin 23 mm guns, and a further pair of similar guns in a manually-directed tail turret. Some aircraft were fitted with a single, fixed gun in the starboard side of the nose. The Mya-4 was equipped for in-flight refuelling, and possessed an intercontinental range with a conventional or nuclear bomb load, but it is not thought to have been built in large numbers for the strategic bomber role, in which it was code-named Bison-A. During the late 'fifties, Bison-A began to be used as a flight refuelling tanker.

From 1964, units of the A-VMF (Soviet Naval Aviation) introduced a maritime reconnaissance version (Bison-B). This version, sometimes referred to as the Mya-4A, was still in use in 1974, when the total number of Bisons in service (including tankers) was estimated at about eighty-five. Bison-B can be distinguished from Bison-A by its solid, radar-carrying nose, numerous under-fuselage electronics bulges, and deletion of the rear dorsal and ventral gun positions.

As early as 1959 a series of international speed-with-payload and height-with-payload records were set up by Myasishchev aircraft designated 103-M and 201-M, powered by D-15 turbojet engines. The 103-M is now thought to have been a variant of the Bison-B; but not until 8 years later did one of these aircraft appear in public, when a single 201-M was exhibited at the Aviation Day display at Domodedovo in July 1967. It was then immediately apparent that this was a progressive development of the Bison-B, from which it differed principally (apart from the change of powerplant) in having an extended and redesigned nose section, incorporating a fixed flight-refuelling probe and radar and electronic equipment; and modified wings of greater span. This aircraft forms the subject of the colour illustration. The service equivalent of the 201-M is designated Bison-C by NATO. Like the Tu-16, some Bison-Cs have been used to refuel other aircraft of the same type.

75 Lockheed C-141A StarLifter

The first jet aircraft designed from the outset as a military cargo aeroplane, the StarLifter's purpose is to provide fast transportation over global ranges for the USAF Military Airlift Command. It is not the largest-capacity US transport, this distinction now belonging to the later C-5A Galaxy, but it is much faster than earlier transport aircraft. This was graphically demonstrated by a C-141A which transported a 50,000 lb (22,680 kg) payload over 7,500 miles (12,070 km), a feat which it accomplished in $18\frac{1}{4}$ flying hours; a similar operation would have taken $30\frac{1}{2}$ hours by Hercules or $41\frac{3}{4}$ hours by Globemaster. An 88,000 lb (39,916 kg) Minuteman container, 154 troops, 127 paratroops, 80 casualty litters with medical staff, or a 94,000 lb (42,638 kg) cargo load, are all within the StarLifter's capacity; and the aircraft can be unloaded, re-loaded and ready for take-off in less than half an hour. A flight crew of 4 is carried, together with a relief crew for very long range missions. The C-141A was declared the winner of a USAF design competition in March 1961, and the first of five development aircraft was flown on 17 December 1963. Production C-141As became operational with the 44th and 75th Air Transport Squadrons of Military Airlift Command in 1965, and in August of that year were operating in Vietnam. One hundred and thirty-two C-141As were ordered initially by the US Air Force, a reduction on the original requirement due to procurement of the giant C-5A to follow in the late 1960s; but this was later increased to a total of two hundred and eighty-five, which equipped fourteen MAC squadrons. Production was completed in late 1967.

76 Lockheed C-5 Galaxy

Currently the world's largest military transport aircraft, and exceeded in size and gross weight only by later models of the commercial Boeing 747, the Galaxy came into being as the result of the CX-4 requirement issued by the USAF's Military Air Transport Service (now Military Airlift Command) in 1963 for a large logistics transport aircraft. This and other requirements were subsequently combined in a revised requirement, CX-HLS (Cargo Experimental-Heavy Logistics System), for which Boeing, Douglas and Lockheed were invited in 1964 to develop their initial designs further. At the same time, General Electric and Pratt & Whitney were invited to develop an appropriate powerplant for the aircraft. By the end of 1965 the choice had been made of a Lockheed/General Electric association to proceed to the hardware stage with what was then known officially as the C-5A Galaxy. Eight test and evaluation aircraft were built, construction beginning in August 1966 and being followed by the flight of the first Galaxy (66-8303) on 30 June 1968. All eight aircraft were assigned to the flight test programme, which extended into mid-1971. Some eighteen months before this, however, the first of eighty-one

production C-5As had been delivered to the USAF, on 17 December 1969. The USAF has four operational Galaxy squadrons, and the first two of these, based at Charleston AFB, South Carolina, and Travis AFB, California, were already carrying out regular operations to and from Southeast Asia and Europe by mid-1971. The third squadron was also based at Travis AFB, and the fourth at Dover AFB, Delaware.

An important factor in the CX-HLS specification was that the Galaxy should, despite its greater size, be capable of operating from the same 8,000 ft (2,440 m) runways as the C-141 StarLifter, and of landing on semi-prepared runways of no more than 4,000 ft (1,220 m) in combat areas. To distribute runway load, the Galaxy has a 28-wheel landing gear, consisting of a 4-wheel nose unit and four 6-wheel main bogies. It carries a normal crew of 5, with a rest area at the front of the upper deck for up to 15 people, including a relief crew. The interior is divided into forward and rear upper compartments and a single lower deck, total volume of all three compartments being 42,825 cu ft (1,212·7 cu m). The C-5A is intended primarily as a freighter, in which role typical loads may include two M-60 tanks or sixteen 15 cwt lorries; or one M-60, two Iroquois helicopters, five M-113 personnel carriers, one M-59 2½ ton truck and an M-151 5 cwt truck; or ten Pershing missiles with their towing and launching vehicles; or thirty-six standard load pallets.

Straight-in cargo loading can be accomplished via the upward-hinged nose and the rear-fuselage ramp/door, simultaneously if necessary. If required as a personnel transport, the C-5A can carry 75 troops on the rear upper deck and 270 on the lower deck. In early 1975 the Imperial Iranian Air Force was expected to order ten Galaxies.

77 General Dynamics (Convair) B-58 Hustler

Although outweighed in sheer numbers by the larger aeroplane by more than seven to one, the Hustler's designed purpose was to form, with the Boeing Stratofortress, the front-line retaliation force of the USAF's Strategic Air Command. The Command received its first B-58A in March 1960, somewhat more than three years after the type began flight testing, and the last of the eighty-six production B-58As built was delivered in October 1962. From these SAC maintained an operations-ready force of about eighty Hustlers, assigned to the 43rd and 305th Bomb Wings based in the USA. The thirty evaluation aircraft included two XB-58 prototypes (first flight 11 November 1956), eleven YB-58A for service test, and one NB-58A engine testbed. Ten of these thirty aircraft were brought up to production B-58A standard in 1961, and eight others were converted to TB-58A combat trainers. The Hustler was the world's first supersonic strategic bomber, and established nearly a score of world speed and payload/altitude records. It had an unrefuelled range of some 2,000 miles (3,220 km), and over even longer ranges with the use of in-flight refuelling could maintain average speeds in excess of 1,000 mph (1,610 km/hr). A 3-seater, the Hustler had no internal weapons bay, having been designed as a complete weapons system with an under-fuselage 'mission pod' which formed part of the overall area-ruling of the aircraft in its fully-equipped condition. The lower half of the pod contained fuel, which was used first and then jettisoned; the upper half of the pod contained either bombs, camera packs or ECM equipment. As an alternative to the pod, four small-size nuclear weapons could be carried under the centre of the fuselage. The Hustler's internal equipment included a high degree of automated target location and weapon direction systems; a complete ejection capsule for each member of the crew; and a radar-aimed Vulcan multi-barrel 20 mm cannon in the tail-cone for rearward defence. All Hustlers were withdrawn from front-line USAF service in 1970.

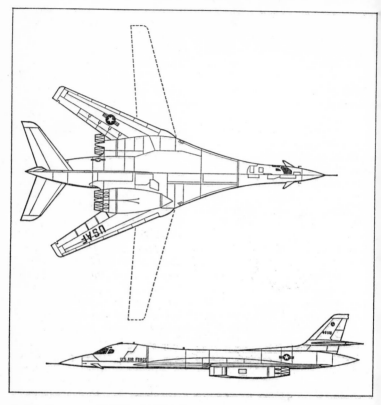

Engines: Four approx. 30,000 lb. (13,610 kg.) s.t. General Electric YF101-GE-100 afterburning turbofans. *Span (wings forward):* 136 ft. 8½ in. (41·67 m.). *Span (wings swept):* 78 ft. 2½ in. (23·84 m.). *Length:* 143 ft. 3½ in. (43·68 m.). *Height.* 33 ft. 7¼ in. (10·24 m.). *Maximum take-off weight:* 389,800 lb. (176,810 kg.). *Maximum speed:* approx. 1,320 m.p.h. (2,125 km./hr.) at 50,000 ft. (15,240 m.). *Maximum range on internal fuel:* 6,100 miles (9,815 km.).

Scheduled as the replacement for Strategic Air Command's B-52 strategic bomber force in the late 1970s, the B-1 made its first flight on 23 December 1974. Three flying prototypes have been ordered. A production decision is not due to be made until 1976, but the USAF requirement is for about 240 aircraft. Nuclear and conventional weapons, including the Boeing SRAM and the new BDM, can be carried in three internal weapon bays and on four under-fuselage stations.

INDEX

The reference numbers refer to the illustrations and corresponding text.

157